Advance Praise for *Booby-Trapped*

"...an outstanding work, a courageous project. This book is required reading for every woman—and the men who love them. It is a brilliant exposé by one savvy woman. The message will capture your attention, tickle your funny bone and satisfy your curiosity."

—Patricia Love, Ed.D., coauthor of *The Emotional Incest Syndrome, Hot Monogamy;* author of *The Truth about Love*

"...each chapter provides a new adventure into the world of therapy and women's issues."

—Cindy Rogers, coauthor of *As I Journey On; Meditations*

"...through her observations, insights, and research, Dr. Sachs uncovers the delicate underpinnings that have held so many women hostage by their body image and kept their partners shut out from understanding them."

—Dr. Dan & Meg Haycraft, founders of TWOgether, Inc., resource for couples education

"...exciting, funny, and emotional. This book should become both a play and a movie-of-the-week. Like *The Vagina Monologues*, once I began to read it, I couldn't put it down."

—Yenny Nun, entertainment reporter, producer, and screenwriter

"...an incredible, important, worthy work for women. Congratulations!"

—Naomi Rhode, CSP, CPAE, 97 Cavett Award Recipient, past president, National Speakers Association

"...a powerful indictment of our breast-obsessed culture delivered through a series of gripping stories of women coming to terms with their bodies and each other."

—William J. Doherty, Ph.D., professor of Family Social Science, University of Minnesota, author of *Take Back Your Marriage: Sticking Together in a World That Pulls Us Apart*

"...having seen multitudes of women in the fitness industry, I realize that a sensation of shame about the breasts is a consistent phenomenon even when the rest of the body is in good physical shape. Reading *Booby-Trapped* has opened my eyes to see solutions for that dichotomy for many women."

—Nicole Parks, M.S., exercise physiologist, NASM-CPT

"...describes the extraordinary significance of women's experiences of their breasts and their bosom's direct impact on female self-esteem and sense of femininity."

—Lori Gordon, Ph.D., author of *Passage to Intimacy*;
founder of PAIRS Programs (Practical Application
of Intimate Relationship Skills)

"...more than breasts or body image, this book is about identity and relationships and self-acceptance. Men can learn a lot about women and their own attitudes about loving the whole person, not a collection of body parts."

—Joan Weiss, Ph.D., clinical psychologist,
expert on women and shame

"...reading about the variety of attitudes these women have toward their breasts opened my eyes. Nili's sensitivity in bringing the issues to the surface warmed my heart."

—Barbara Patton, writer/editor

"...the diverse group of women portrayed in *Booby-Trapped* provides a fascinating look into the fears, loves, and self-esteem issues women have with their own bodies."

—Pam Krank, co-president, Minnesota Chapter,
National Association of Women Business Owners

"...explores the psychological significance attached to breasts as well as the immense role that culture plays to influence women's attitudes about their breasts."

—Uzzi Reiss, M.D.,OB/GYN, author of *Natural*
Hormone Balance for Women

"…a wonderful read, filled with real people, that helps each of us understand more of who we are—and why. I read it in one sitting—how could you ever put *this* book down?

— **Betsy Buckley,** APR, president, What Matters

"…this book appeals to everyone! It is so readable and inform-ative…it really made me think!"

— **Christine Hardten,** a mother of two girls

"…it is a wake-up call for parents and professionals who care about the fragile fabric of a healthy body image, whether for a cherished child, an adolescent, or a woman."

— **Pamela Hartman,** El.Ed. Early Childhood Education

"…there is not a girl over 14 or a woman of any age who will not find this fascinating book tremendously enlightening. I felt the lights going on in my mind with every page. The format which takes us into the group therapy sessions in each chapter is brilliant.

Not only should you own this book, you will want to give a copy to all of the women in your life."

— **Dottie Walters CSP**, Publisher SHARING IDEAS SPEAKERS MAGAZINE, Author; *Speak & Grow Rich*

"…with tenderness, humor and sensitivity, *Booby-Trapped* is the first book of its kind to realistically describe the breast can-cer experience as it relates to women's overall body images. Dr. Nili encourages women to seek out the very factors that can lead them through this experience: psychotherapy, support groups, and the power of positive thinking. *Booby-Trapped* should be required reading for anyone whose life has been touched by breast cancer."

— **Christine K. Clifford, CSP;** author of *Not Now…I'm Having a No Hair Day!* and *Cancer Has Its Privileges: Stories of Hope & Laughter;* CEO/President of The Cancer Club

BOOBY-TRAPPED™

How to Feel Normal
in a Breast-Obsessed World™

Nili Sachs, Ph.D.

Beaver's Pond Press, Inc.
Edina, Minnesota

The characters described in this book are composites of a myriad of individuals I have known over the years. Their names, occupations, physical characteristics, and personal stories have all been rearranged for confidentiality.

ISBN 1-931646-45-7

Library of Congress Catalog Number: 2003101691

Book design and typesetting: Mori Studio
Cover design and illustration: Jaana Bykonich

Printed in the United States of America

Beaver's Pond Press, Inc.

7104 Ohms Lane Suite 216
Edina, MN 55439
(952) 829-8818
www.beaverspondpress.com

This book is lovingly dedicated to
my husband, Ben,
whose support has been nurturing,
like warm milk.

Contents

Acknowledgments

These people have been the wind beneath my wings.

Sarah Wintraub
Bat-Sheva Goldstein
Alina and Edan Shalev
Guy Shalev
Udi Goldstein
Orit Katz
Libby and Shira Goldstein
Abigail Lubliner
Yael and Uzzi Reiss, M.D.
Barbara McNichol
William J. Doherty, Ph.D.
Lori Gordon, Ph.D.
Patricia Love, Ph.D.
Yenny Nun
Dan Haycraft, M.D.
Meg Haycraft, MSW
Joan Weiss, Ph.D.
David Martin
Cindy Rogers
Pam Hartman
Betsy Buckley
Nicole Parks, MS
Pam Krank
John Kremer
Milt Adams
Jaana Bykonich
Jack Caravela
Greg Godek
Naomi Rhode, CSP, CPAE
Christine Hardten
Arelene Vernon

And my patients/students during the past three decades.

Preface

I simply had to write this book.

First, women patients and women friends were curiously noticing other women's breast sizes and shapes. Their comments sounded like a murmur or a mumble or a gossip, but not yet as a cultural pressure.

That was twenty years ago.

Later in my career, those whispers found a strong voice. I actually heard in the privacy of my office women's complaints about one's unlucky body, poor presentation of femininity, abandonment by God, shameful self, feeling nature's cruelty, and more phrases that clearly indicated misery had company.

Recently I observed further deterioration on this theme: women blaming what was happening in their intimate relationships on their breast size and shape. Worse yet, single women blaming their breasts for not getting the "right" dates! Some examples:

- *A woman I've known for some time got divorced and started dating. She had her breasts enhanced surgically "so I can get a richer husband next time around."*

- *A married man confided in me saying he is no longer attracted to his wife, the mother of their three children, as her breasts looked "somewhat" sagging.*

- *A first-grade teacher would not breast-feed her newborn declaring, "My husband does not want my breasts ruined forever…"*

- *Another woman in her thirties felt self-conscious about the asymmetry of her breasts, so she had them equalized by inserting an implant into one of them. Once she got married, she decided to keep the procedure a secret from her new husband. It is still secret years into the marriage…*

- *The husband of a friend of mine left his marriage as soon as he heard his wife was diagnosed with breast cancer.*

At first I thought I wanted to write Booby-Trapped *as an educational tool to decode some issues regarding intimate relationships. Then one day, one of my six nieces (I have two sons, one grandson, no nephews) told me about a classmate, 14 years old, who is saving "all" the money she makes from babysitting(!) for the purpose of having a "boob job" at age 16. I cringed at that thought and asked my niece to find out if the classmate's parents know and/or what do they have to say about it. I got the answer the next day: her parents will match the savings, and by her Sweet 16th birthday, they will help her find a surgeon.*

What were they thinking?

I learned that Booby-Trapped *is not only a relationship issue; it's a cultural outcry!*

At that moment I felt I simply had to write this book.

*Size and Shape are Human Tissues.
Shame and Fear are Human Issues!*

—from *Treasured Chest,* by Nili Sachs, Ph.D.

*If femininity means female sexuality and its
loveliness, women never lost it and do not
need to buy it back.*

—from *The Beauty Myth,* by Naomi Wolf.

THE FEMALE BREAST IS THE ONE HUMAN ORGAN THAT IS MOST constantly subjected to physical changes during an adult's lifetime. This perfectly normal phenomenon has a purpose; each physical change in the adult female's breast assists in a particular stage of life. Therefore, changes in breast size, shape, and texture exist for a reason. The psychological significance attached to these changes is apparently greater than the physical changes themselves.

Many women treat their breasts (if they do not like them) as foreign objects. Society is only too happy to play along with their frustrations. Men's magazines and Madison Avenue advertising tell their readers what is chic and acceptable. That breasts must be larger, smaller, perkier, more symmetrical—are among the various messages we get.

This phenomenon is not new to most women, nor was it new to me. **What's new is the amount of time, effort, money, and thought so many women spend "dealing" with their breasts.**

During women's group therapy, marital therapy sessions, and seminars, I've discovered four specific concerns: First, women's deep emotional investment in size and shape of their breasts. Second, their vulnerability to aesthetic cultural ideals. Third, and in particular, their entrapment by their own perceptions of femininity and eroticism. Fourth, women of all ages and backgrounds were blaming several intimacy issues not working in their lives on the shapes and sizes of their breasts.

Do modern women regard their breasts as a vital part of what they understand femininity to be? Or do they react to men's fantasies about what is attractive? Is the preoccupation with breast size and shape a response to the media bombardment of "enhancing breasts" industries? Why do so many women today lack a positive relationship with their breasts?

Booby-Trapped illuminates this vulnerability and entrapment. Yet, it is so much more than that. **It is an emotional self-examination of women's breasts.** And it is also the first relationship guide to female breasts, not only for women but for the men who love them.

Booby-Trapped is structured as a series of women's group sessions. Why? Because women tend to get the information they need for personal growth through their involvement in these groups. They talk to other women, share experiences, readings, and a myriad of information, and then openly discuss the ramifications of an issue.

I will introduce you to ten women and the concerns that have been brought up in my psychotherapy group sessions. These women aren't real people. Each one is a composite of the countless women who have articulated these concerns time and time again in group sessions and seminars.

This guide explores the growing care and intimacy women develop as they gather for sessions in my office, a safe haven for honest and open discussions. They reveal a typically modern preoccupation with self-esteem, femininity, and body image, particularly related to their breasts. You will quite possibly see yourself in the characteristics of one or more of these women.

MEDIUM OF EXPRESSION

I believe there is certain logic in our need to manipulate or modify the shape of our breasts. The human body has continually been put to use as a medium for the expression of cultural, tribal, or genealogical needs. There is a tendency for nations, tribes, and other groups to demand that their members reflect a uniformity— a sameness, an ideal—in their physical appearance. Extreme exceptions in individual appearances are looked down upon; the "different one" can be forced to alter his or her appearance or even be expelled from the group. Many civilizations have attempted, at one time or another, to force some form of body manipulation or shape alteration on some of their members, often at a heavy price. The physical pain, the lifelong suffering, and the emotional consequences of the tortured bodies were often beyond description.

There are health and psychological consequences to using our bodies to express fashion trends or project cultural messages. Using the breasts of the human female to express some fashion and cultural statements is a new twist—not even a hundred years old—to an ancient ritual. An entire chapter in this book is devoted to exploring rituals from non-North American cultures that use the human body as a medium of expression. That's what makes the subject matter so fascinating.

EFFECT OF SAMENESS

Along with the women in this book, you will discover these body manipulations and more as you search to understand people's perceptions of sameness, tradition, and fashions—and experience belonging to a particular identity group. This book clearly shows how the need for sameness profoundly affects our modern life.

ATTITUDE OF FEMININITY

Booby-Trapped also addresses issues of femininity as complex clusters of human behaviors and attitudes. These attitudes get assigned at birth. "It's a girl" or "It's a boy" are lifelong commitments to differentiate and distinguish particular ways of behavior. Parents, brothers, husbands, or other male friends play a major role in how women react to their own bodies—and specifically their breasts—in spite of themselves. You'll see how some of the women in this book literally fall into a "man-made" trap.

BREAST IMPLANTS

Any book about breasts cannot ignore breast implants. *Booby-Trapped* discusses the profound course of psychological rebuilding in the aftermath of breast cancer. It addresses the controversy surrounding implants, whether for cosmetic or healing reasons.

However, *Booby-Trapped* does not make a statement against breast implants.

Each of us knows at least one survivor of breast cancer who chose reconstructive surgery using breast implants. These women have heroic stories to tell and hundreds of survivors praise breast implants!

"RECOVERY" AFTER BREAST-FEEDING

Following the era in which the breast became a "status symbol," a second generation of mothers are showing serious concerns regarding the effects of breast-feeding on the shape, form, and beauty of their breasts. We "judge" a woman's breasts after she has breast-fed: Are they still a "10"? A "9"? Can she "recover" their initial shape?

NEW WAY TO APPRECIATE BREASTS

This guide gives you a way to build a new appreciation for every woman's relationship with her breasts. The women you'll read about grapple with identification, approval, and disapproval of their own attitudes and understanding. You can acquire that same knowledge as you work through the questions and issues posed in the last chapter.

CHARACTER INDEX

For your convenience, you'll find a Character Index at the end of the book. It points to pages where each character's story unfolds. Using the Character Index, you can follow the psychological journey of any character you choose.

I wish you joy in discovering a healthy relationship with your breasts and those of the women you love!

Chapter One

SIZE
is Everything!

Meeting Number 12 of a Women's Therapy Group

Our breasts are the part of our anatomy most identified with nurturing. And they are also perhaps the most highly charged area of our bodies, flagrantly exploited by the culture we live in as our most potent weapon in the battle to win the love and approval of a man.

> —From *The Wisdom of Menopause,*
> by Christiane Northrup, M.D.

The products that find their way to female chests—falsies and wired bras, creams and lotions, breast implants and nipple rings (why not rouge or tattoos?)—keep the wheels of business rolling and feed the fantasies of countless women and men, for whom the breast merits all the enhancement and the attention it can get.

> —from *A History of the Breast,*
> by Marilyn Yalom

"SIZE IS EVERYTHING!" LISA'S COMMENT WAS GREETED WITH silence from the other nine women in the group. "All these last years," she continued, "I spent worrying about my breast size in comparison to others." The silence this time was punctuated by nods from many of the others. "I feel that sexuality was sort of numb in me until now," Lisa continued. This time she elicited more than nods.

Beth shook her head which caused her close-cropped, salt-and-pepper hair to move in dismay and opened her mouth to speak, but caught herself before she said how strongly she disagreed with Lisa—particularly with her values. The older woman's experiences had long ago taught her not to depend on external appearances. Looking around, realizing she was outnumbered, Beth smiled and said, "I guess I'll keep it for later. I need to be more tolerant with things I see and hear." Leaning closer to Lisa, she said softly, "I want to fix you and help you without considering if you are ready to be helped."

"That was a mouthful, Beth," said Tina, the elegant Japanese-American woman, in a voice that held a touch of sarcasm. "I had no idea," Tina continued, "that you were aware of the overmothering you do to Lisa. I'm glad you can wait this time. I actually want to hear what Lisa has to say. I happen to feel just like she does." The sarcasm left her voice, replaced with a touch of sadness. I made a mental note of it, but decided not to interrupt the process.

"You've heard me talking about my daughter, Amy," said Grace, the oldest group member. "Every time you bring up the smallness of your breasts, Lisa, I picture Amy, who is built just like you. And like you, she is preoccupied with breast size. And like you, she keeps shopping around for plastic surgeons. I'm as scared for her as I am for you. What can possibly develop from this obsession? I don't even want to imagine it. But I want to hear you out. I'm eager for new information. I don't mean to sound contradictory. On the one hand, I'm opposed to what you're saying, but I'm also learning from it. Maybe I'll get to understand my Amy. Please continue. You look so excited." Rosie, the nurse's aide, agreed.

"You are more hyper than usual; you're actually on the edge of your seat." She paused and shifted her bulk awkwardly in her chair. "I also want to ask why you haven't been at the last two meetings. You've never missed one before."

"I wanted to ask you that too," said Pat, who was dressed in sporty tweeds and seemed to be more engaged, more forthcoming than in previous meetings.

"So, it looks like this is Lisa's session," Isabel laughed, adjusting her large, brightly patterned scarf around her suit. After the others had joined in, she turned to Lisa.

"Now, what is on your mind anyway?"

"Breasts," Lisa answered with a smile.

"I'd do anything for a bigger breast size," Rosie said, wistfully.

"Of course," said Isabel. "Boobs and more boobs. How could I forget? Well, Lisa, you have the floor."

"Go for it, Lisa," Angela said. "Unload yourself." The tall, beautiful black woman unbuttoned her navy double-breasted jacket and shrugged it off to reveal her long, thin arms.

Lisa looked at all of them and then burst out, "Sexy! That's what I want to be. And I am going to be sexy if it kills me!" There were giggles from some of the women; one or two raised their eyebrows, either from Lisa's vehemence or in alarm.

"But you've heard me say that so many times," Lisa paused. "Well, enough said, I'm here today to show you my victory!" With that, she stood up, almost defiantly. "I've been planning this for a few years now. Look what I've got." She began to unbutton her blouse. "For the first time in my life, I'm normal, I am sexy. I can't wait to show you." Lisa deftly peeled off her red shirt to reveal a lacy, Victoria's Secret black bra just barely covering two large white mounds.

Beth shrieked.

Rosie gasped.

Others giggled.

And Tina let out a "Wow."

Then there was that silence.

Lisa removed her bra slowly, deliberately, and just stood there for what seemed like an eternity. No one could take her eyes off of Lisa or more precisely, her breasts, which dominated her once small-breasted frame. Her breasts paraded the room, front and center, greeting more than one pair of envious eyes.

I must confess, while Lisa was exposing her new body parts, I did nothing. I was in shock. I am an experienced psychotherapist, a professional. I was trained to keep the focus on the patients—not just one patient—but all of them. Here were ten women of different ages and backgrounds—professionally, ethnically, racially, and in attitude—I was speechless. And I was blushing.

I was blushing as one of my patients—half naked!—strutted her stuff before all of us. Our reactions were honest and emotionally self-exposing. I had to remind myself that I was the therapist, leader, educator, and just as important, boundaries-keeper. My immediate reaction was, well, primitive: I was embarrassed—for both Lisa and the others. I had not anticipated this, nor had I reacted firmly enough when it happened. My blushing gave me plenty of data about the moment, especially about myself as a person; I was unprepared to expose certain emotions—my own.

But what were they? I usually kept my below-the-surface emotions buried beneath my professional mask. The first set of emotions was a combination of envy, excitement, and vulnerability. I was feeling just a bit out of control. The only good that came of this, I thought at the time, was knowing that I got all of this vital information from one silly blush. Thinking back, another set of my emotions was emerging: sexual excitement, anxiety about Lisa's conduct, and the reactions of the women in the room. How will I contain them?

The commotion in the room gave me time not only to collect myself but also to observe the others in our surroundings. The space in which we held these weekly meetings was my office, located on the north side of Wilshire Boulevard in the heart of Beverly Hills, California. The building itself had seven floors; my office occupied a suite on the fourth floor.

There was a waiting room behind door #402. Three armchairs and one love seat occupied the waiting area. There was no receptionist, no phones or charts in the area. The sitting corner had a few plants and some modern art posters. The magazines on the coffee table featured themes such as family life, nutrition, and travel.

An internal door divided the waiting room from the actual office. When a patient arrived, she or he touched a small light switch, which lit inside the office. This was my signal that a patient had arrived for an appointment. (Knocking on the door is not customary in the mental health industry.) This particular office was furnished especially for group meetings. The crux of office furniture consisted of eleven wheeled chairs, equal in size. I wanted the participants to have freedom of movement, the ability to get closer or farther away from each other (thus the reason for the wheels). In my experience, when one is mobile, it is easier to read an individual's body language.

One display in the office, however, was personal to me: a collection of tissue boxes of many styles, textures, and colors. They were placed on a long shelf near the ceiling. Each box came from a different city—or a different state of mind.

As for the members of the group, they range in age from the early twenties to sixties, and all are Americans. Their various backgrounds include differences in education, religion, experiences of therapy, marital and family status, energy levels, body sizes and shapes, and aspirations. A diversity lab.

1. First, there is **Lisa**, our proud peacock—or peahen. She is 24 going on 17, single, blonde, slender, her body taut from hours of

weekly exercise, and most assuredly provocative. The "baby" of her family, she was doted on by her baby-boomer parents who owned a trendy restaurant in Studio City, a fashionable area of greater Los Angeles. In high school, Lisa was a star cheerleader and became the hostess of her parents' restaurant, where she learned to cater to—and yearned to be like—the patrons. She still sees herself as worthy of everyone's attention. Her ambition is to be an actress, but so far she has only landed a few local commercials and voice assignments for books on tape. Developmentally, she is at the edge of discovering erotic adult feelings, which she calls "dirty little secrets that feel good."

Self-centered, lacking boundaries, playful, and energetic, her youthful behavior threatens others. There is a core of softness in her, however, giving her the ability to express empathy and forgiveness for others and herself. For now, she is simply acting immaturely with her focus on "getting" from life, including applause. She is dating, although her goal is not intimacy but admiration. Lisa lives her life through trial and error.

2. **Beth**, age 48, but looking several years older, is a mature and down-to-earth mother figure to the group. Intelligent, educated, married to an protestant clergyman, she volunteers for many social causes. Beth has a certain quality that stands out from the rest: she lovingly accepts her body and her looks, including her so-called imperfections. Beth is at the extreme opposite from Lisa on the continuum—in maturity, materialism, and spirituality. Beth—morally sure and opinionated, yet tolerant—still needs to learn to let go of control in her emotional life. With Lisa, in particular, whom she constantly "corrects," and the others, she has her hands full. She wants to teach them, to lecture them, to tell them right from wrong.

3. **Rosie**, age 34, is an injured bird. Brown hair and brown eyes. It would be hard to tell what Rosie's body shape is or how she looks in fitted cloths. She is usually wearing oversize sweats and no-structure outfits. Rosie talks about her need to lose weight.

For now she might be slightly overweight. In her general appearance, though, she is somewhat frumpy.

Rosie was born in Mexico City of Hispanic parents. After her father's death and her mother's new marriage, the family immigrated to Los Angeles where they sought work in the garment industry. They prospered and branched out, building their own small factory. Now they also run a retail shop, which provides them with a comfortable living. Rosie is a nurse's aide and has recently begun attending school part-time to study nutrition. She wishes to build a new career and lose weight in the process.

Rosie is extremely defensive and suppressed to the point of self-deprecation; she is consumed with other women's looks and attractiveness. Rosie exposes her obsession with her older sister, Gail, claiming she was unloved in comparison to Gail. The ugly face of jealousy, in several of its forms is introduced to the group by her. Rosie is envious to the extent of being paralyzed socially. She has never been in an intimate relationship and does not feel she deserves to be loved.

4. **Grace**, at 64, is the oldest member of the group. Grace was born in Toronto, Canada, and arrived with her parents in California at age fourteen. She is a retired social worker who brings to our process some outstanding research that she discovers in her readings. Emotionally, Grace shows a lack of acceptance toward her femininity and sensuality. She appears as a contradiction: a knowledgeable person, an expert in many areas, yet lacking an ability to trust the other in intimate relationship.

Widowed for several years, Grace must deal with a number of issues. She was forced to declare bankruptcy after her husband, a prosperous manager of a department store, died. Then she discovered a reality he had not been truthful about.

5. **Pat**, age 36, is a sales associate in real estate. She is a person of low self-esteem who keeps herself living in the past. Pat is the only group member who didn't show any interest in Lisa's breasts at first.

Pat was referred to the group by a grief therapist who had observed that her grief over the death of her mother had become pathological. She idealizes the alliance between herself and her mother, Susan. Pat adored her mother's strength, resolve, and talents.

Pat suffers from severe mood swings. We have noticed that when she is depressed she'll come in to a meeting looking like she'd just gotten out of bed. On an up-swing mood, she'll walk in tall, professionally dressed, and willingly contribute to the process.

6. **Katherine**, age 39, is a widowed pediatrician. Her medical knowledge of the human body provides both an endless amount of information and a reality check for the group. She deeply appreciates prevention and will teach the others to be proactive. She is pragmatic, assertive, and empathic toward others. From her medical training, she has developed an approach to life that is scientific, logical, and rational. She admits, however, that she has become somewhat desensitized to life experiences such as intimacy and the natural fun of being a female. Despite her profession—or because of it, which keeps consuming her—her body looks slightly worn: below her waist she is round from her hips to her ankles. Her arms are thin, however, and her hands are exquisite like those of a surgeon's or a concert pianist's.

7. **Angela**, age 31, is one of the most thought-provoking members of the group. She is a black career woman in an era that respects successful black women. An accomplished model, she inspires many young women. She presents herself as an aware, feminine, and helpful person. Angela is married to Jim, a successful attorney for a Hollywood studio. Jim was also a model when he was younger.

Angela likes the group process as a tool to look inside herself. Her main goal is to improve her intimate relationship with her husband Jim. He refuses to partake in marriage therapy; therefore she joins the group for her personal growth.

8. **Isabel**, age 29, provides one of the most dramatic stories of the group. She is an intelligent, sophisticated world traveler, a graphic designer. She has recently expanded her business and hired more designers to assist her in developing corporate identity programs for major corporations.

Isabel is a well-rounded person, the Swiss-born daughter of an American diplomat father. Isabel's mother devoted herself to the family, instilling in her daughter many positive characteristics. Isabel is a child of nature with a sweet disposition. She is uninhibited both emotionally and physically. Her exposure to the wide world has left an impression on her personal taste. Isabel stands out in her appearance, from her clothes to her shiny raven hair that is cut perfectly to frame her attractive face. Isabel is friendly and caring. Her expressions of warmth and empathy flow out of her with ease.

9. **Jane**, age 55, took a legal secretary course after high school because her attorney father and her mother thought this was the right thing to do. They advised her to find a "nice Jewish man to marry." She did find that nice man, Alan, also a lawyer, of course. Jane also found she was good at her work and loved it. Now the administrator of a law firm that has grown to more than 120 lawyers, she is comfortable with her life. She also takes on a mother's role with the attorneys in her firm. Jane helps instruct the new people to ease their negotiations through the civil courts and occasionally rewrites their briefs. She has been rewarded with significant raises throughout the years. She drives a vintage Cadillac sporting a license plate that reads MOM LAW—a gift from the attorneys in her firm.

She is the mother of two daughters who have married successful men and moved across the country. They return home with the grandchildren for the high holy days.

Jane provides background noise to the content of the group. Most psychotherapy groups I have witnessed have a "Jane" member in them. This member does not contribute much to the group, and appears to take away as little as possible. Just as she is *there* for her attorneys, she is *there* for the women's needs. Often, she yields her time to others who want the floor, thinking that their needs are more important than her own. However, a marital crisis brings her to the forefront of the group's work. She will increasingly shed inhibitions as she sheds pounds, in an attempt to recapture, if not her marriage, then her sense of womanhood.

10. **Tina**, age 41, is elegant, assertive, prosperous, witty, and ageless looking. She was born in Japan to Japanese parents. Her father was a businessman whose work brought him and his family to the United States. He would leave them for weeks, providing plenty of cash but no guidance. Tina learned to appreciate financial independence. She soon began to anticipate her private American dream. She earned her MBA and surpassed her father in her success as the CEO of her own marketing research firm. Tina has been taught since childhood that things made in America are worth striving to obtain. One of her acquisitions was Chad, one of her top executives who became her husband. The marriage lasted less than two years, although Chad remains at his post, since he is a most valuable employee. "I cut my losses in the personal relationship," she says, "but recognized he was still highly productive as a manager."

This describes the women who witnessed Lisa's—more—than psychological exposure.

It is extremely unusual, in the process of most psychotherapy group settings, to promote or tolerate or use any kind of physical undressing. In my entire career, I can only count a handful of experiences when serious professionals have used the naked body as any part of a treatment. What comes to mind are several therapeutic massage classes and a series of Bioenergetic therapy sessions. In these situations the treatment technique calls for deep breathing and observation of energy flow, preferably wearing underwear. Yet here I was, with this new behavior on my lap, or as Lisa would say, "in my face."

I watched the spontaneity and joy in this historic meeting with growing interest. Several years ago, I would have called this undressing behavior "acting out." I would have been more judgmental and threatened that my professionalism had been compromised. I would have wondered if I or my group was out of control.

Now, the room was energized like never before. The behavior might still be called acting out; the group and I might still be out of control. Yet we trusted—at least I did—that everything could be verbalized and, therefore, dealt with appropriately.

"Is it hot in here or is it me?" asked Grace.

"You may feel a little hot," Lisa said, picking up her cue, "but I am a hot mama!" We all laughed loud and hard—a bit more, perhaps, than the joke deserved. It was a good way to work through that significant moment of anxiety. It's over, I thought. We had survived another major hurdle as a group.

Weeks before, Katherine, the physician and excellent source of medical information, had presented a book to the group. In her extensive and very informative book *Women's Bodies, Women's Wisdom,* Dr. Christiane Northrup writes,

> I believe many people when they were children didn't get nearly the ideal amount of contact with mothers' breast; too many of us have been nurtured not by maternal breasts but by cold, plastic nipples and chemical formula made by multinational corporations. No wonder our society is hung up on the female breast! No wonder the stage gets set so early for distress in this area of the female body!

Just three or four meetings before this historic one, Katherine brought Dr. Northrup's book along and read some citations to the group. She handed it to Tina who promised to return the precious resource and pass it on to Pat, and so on. The women love to share resources and feel grateful for each other's generosity and ingenuity.

Katherine also read this excerpt from the same book a few weeks ago:

> Most cosmetic breast surgery is undertaken because women feel they don't look as good as the models in magazines or as good as their lovers want them to look, or because our breast-obsessed culture so favors large breasts. This size concern is medicalized in plastic surgery jargon, which writes the indication for breast augmentation as chronic bilateral micromastia. That simply means: two small breasts that have been there for a while.

At that time, this definition evoked some laughter and giggles. Tina reacted by announcing she knew exactly what the Latin terms meant. "Let me rephrase this medical definition to fit my perception," she said. "Not two small breasts but TOO small breasts that have been, etc." We all laughed at her wit.

I noticed at the time, that Lisa's reaction was unlike the others'. She was the only one to speak after Tina's comment. To paraphrase, she said with a smile, "I'll show them." Lisa had already made up her mind to have breast implants and probably had an appointment for the surgical procedure. She did not, however, choose to share it with us before the surgery. She was here now, with us, with her new breasts, living the moment. And she loved it.

I would not have protested Lisa undergoing the surgical procedure. That wasn't my role then nor is it now. As her therapist, my wishes for Lisa are strictly to give her a chance to examine her own motivations—a second glance into the world of her fantasy regarding her sensuality and her measures of attractiveness. That said, I was especially interested in Lisa's expectations after making this major change in her physical, psychological, social, and sexual development.

Psychotherapy groups like this one are about promoting the mental health of their members. We actively explore the evolution of thoughts, perceptions, expectations, feelings, and body images. Group dynamics are, like the name, dynamite! In no time, powerful struggles emerge between perceived norms of femininity and actual images of self, whether it means true self, false self, or borrowed self.

When I announced the opening of this women-only therapy group, I got a good response. Jane, Lisa, Beth, Angela, and Grace had all participated in previous workshops and seminars of mine, and had been interested in women's groups for some time. Isabel and Rosie were encouraged to join the group by friends and family members of other seminar attendees. Katherine, a former member of a different women's group, had actually waited for a new one to start. Tina and Pat were referred by colleagues who had participated in my previous women's groups.

This group has developed a definite, distinct personality in several ways. Most important, BREASTS, as the group theme had been budding—excuse the pun—since the inception of the group. For the first time in my career, breasts were topics of discussion every few weeks. Each group member had an angle on the subject of breasts. Each one wanted to express her views and get feedback. After twelve weeks together, most of us developed an interest and curiosity about breasts, their symbolism and their significance. We finally realized that breast size mattered to our culture. In Lisa's words: Size is everything!

Lisa had joined the group as a fashionable gesture. She wanted it all: to feel loved, to have fame, to enjoy the "fast" life, to have a personal trainer, to dress provocatively, and to have a perfectly sexy body. She heard she'll 'be cool' if she saw a therapist. Lisa was a constant challenge in the group. At the first meeting, she presented us with a reexamination of some truths. Life was good for Lisa, very good. Some of us would have liked to taste just once more the innocence of "a first time": our first true love, our first

French kiss, the first erotic feelings, the first "dirty little secrets that feel good." Lisa's egocentric views made some of us feel like maternal figures or schoolteachers: we wanted to educate and protect her. Still, her constant barrage of youthful energy and youth-like concepts threatened others in the group.

We were able to see how each of us had this "Lisa" part within ourselves. She was a *mirror*. She provided lessons to an entire group of older women. She was a "girly" girl, like some of us actually used to be, or wanted to be. She stimulated our fantasies of living not only as a mother, a spouse, a teacher, or a responsible partner, but also as a feminine woman. How fresh it sounded to most of us.

There she was! Lisa, the girl who wanted to be a woman. One spontaneous movement had produced an ocean full of reactions regarding femininity, sexuality, beauty, attractiveness, health, liberty, and the pursuit of happiness. That same movement also exposed many undercurrents: fear, envy, admiration, power, money, politics, and entrapment.

Lisa's "show and tell" flash was not easy to absorb. Beth, in particular, was shocked and disappointed. As it turned out, fighting against breast implants is her platform! Lisa's new implants represented a great deal of what she objected to in life. Beth felt displeased that Lisa, who seemed to be listening to her all along, made this decision by herself and was flaunting the results "in her face." She was the group's "big mama."

For me, Beth represented a classic generation of social activists, a natural leader, caring and selfless. Beth reminds me of the late clinical social worker Virginia Satir whom I have admired for the last three decades. Beth has a natural love of people, love of truth, and love of God. She has the soul of a volunteer, responsible, modest, with a no-frills personality. No wonder she spoke up first. In this microcosm of society, Beth and Lisa were on opposite ends of the imaginary continuum.

As usual, Grace was trying to say something. However, the others' reactions easily drowned her out. Grace came from Beth's generation, but was out of touch with sensuality and certain pleasures in life. She was also the extreme opposite of Lisa's lifestyle and aspirations. Grace had been the most judgmental of Lisa's behaviors throughout the sessions, more so than the others.

Jane "felt" Grace's opinion coming and asked, "Grace, you look so uncomfortable at this moment. Do you need to say something?" Jane caught Grace by surprise. Grace refused to share what was going on inside her. She looked embarrassed and troubled but said that her concerns could wait until Lisa's "celebration" was over.

Lisa was energized with her new life, her new breasts, and her renewed sexuality. The room was still roaring with voices, energy, admiration, envy, questions, and statements. For this mostly secular group, the name of God was invoked often, but not in ways that showed approval. "Oh, my God," "Lord," "Goodness gracious."

In the next few sessions, the women would find more articulate voices to express their opinions, and they would not be shy about their reactions to what Lisa had done to her body, nor what her actions represented to each of them. Yet, for the moment, none would be able to clearly reflect what it meant to them.

Chapter Two

What a LIFT!

Later in the Same Meeting

If breasts could talk, they would probably tell jokes—every light-bulb joke in the book.

—from *Woman,* by Natalie Angier

In a culture in which women and men alike are brought up on Barbie dolls, Miss America pageants, and Playboy images, breasts are a very charged part of our anatomy, both physically and metaphorically.

—from *Women's Bodies, Women's Wisdom,* by Christiane Northrup, M.D.

E WERE OVER STIMULATED. I WAS NOT SURE IF I WANTED TO work more today. I knew that this time had the potential for a good group process to take place. Our defenses were down, uninhibited emotions were flowing, envious feelings and denials were everywhere. What an excellent opportunity for therapy work!

When the women finally settled down and Lisa was packed again into her clothes, Beth spoke. Tears in her eyes and voice quivering, she could not keep her hands still. Momentarily controlling herself, she finally blurted out, "How could you, Lisa? I don't know what to say. I'm so disappointed—and scared. I don't want to rain on your parade, so I'd better stop before I lose control. I feel so angry. You should know better! You are taking a great risk with your health, with your life. There is so much evidence, so much information against implants. I feel so guilty for not informing you while there was still time."

Beth's outburst set off the others, and I formed a stop sign in the air. I was not about to have Lisa—or anyone else, for that matter—launch into a speech on one's rights about free expression. Once I had their attention, I began slowly. "Thank you, Lisa, for sharing," I said in a serious tone. But Lisa chuckled and the group laughed loudly.

"Do you feel a bit naughty?" I asked.

"More like plenty naughty," she answered, grinning.

"Tell us about it, please," I said then and gestured to Beth to give Lisa a chance to elaborate. Beth nodded in agreement and settled back in her chair. Pat brushed her hair back from her face, a constant gesture, and moved uncomfortably about in her seat. Rosie looked impatient. Jane leaned forward and said, "Don't worry, Lisa, we're here for you."

"No," Angela stated abruptly. "We are here for ourselves, but please talk to us anyway."

Finally, Lisa smiled and said, "I'm dying to tell you, since I've missed coming here for the last couple of weeks, and the holiday before that. I haven't seen you for a few weeks now. That time was used for healing and reflecting. I've been thinking about how much I appreciate you. Most of my life, I've felt that I was homely and so plain. Mother Nature made a mistake when my body was developing. Feeling normal became an obsession for me. I thought a lot about this big decision—the biggest in my life. I went for good looks. Actually, I went for the best I can look. I've wanted this since I was sixteen. I wanted more boobs, more sex appeal, more dates, and a little competitive edge as an actress. It's over. I've got my dream.

"So, yes! I do feel naughty. Also, on a serious note, I feel full, satisfied. I'm complete now. You know, I felt this gap between being a girl and being a *woman*."

She looked around at the others. "I'm like you now. Like you, Angela, even if Beth hates me. I want to look good in my clothes. I love my boobs, and they feel so normal. Yeah, I feel normal. I am normal—and more: normal and sexy. And guess what? That guy I met last month, Danny—I told you about him—he is crazy about me now."

We were silent. Lisa lifted a tissue to her eyes, wiped some tears, sat back, and looked around the room. "You guys, I'm so happy to be here today. I could not sleep last night. You have helped me so much. I appreciate you and I wanted to show you the results. Maybe it isn't what Dr. Nili calls group process, but I wanted you to see. And it's okay to have fun, isn't it? I was nervous coming in this evening. I was expecting to defend my actions. I know that you have opinions, information, and that you care. I made a decision to listen to you after my procedure but not before. I have great respect for you and I like to learn, but I didn't want any other influences on me. I didn't want to change my mind." Lisa was looking at Beth, her symbolic mother in the group.

Then I looked at Beth who had been angry about Lisa's outburst. "I know, I know," Beth said. "I've almost ruined it for you. I can't keep quiet when the subject of implants comes up. Look, my friend Nina has implants. They're made of silicone. She talks about it frequently. She showed them to me once. I got scared. She made me put my hand on one of her breasts to see if I could feel the implant. It felt hard and grotesque. Not like human flesh at all. I love my friend Nina and I don't want anything bad to happen to her. We started looking at newspapers and the Internet for information about implants. I don't want to scare you, Lisa, but it is pretty sad," she said and then sighed. "There is some good with the bad, but the news is always about the bad things. I feel scared for young women who don't know all the ramifications. Sorry, Lisa. I see how happy you are. And I do understand why you didn't tell us your plans."

No one interrupted Beth. She can be very charismatic when she gets going. She and her husband, a clergyman, lead a large Christian community. In the past I have worked with them, leading weekend and evening workshops for couples and families. She has always volunteered for social causes, and I thought that she might begin to lecture on her newly found cause against breast implants. But I had yet to voice my idea.

Lisa was so focused on her new look that she was not at all moved by Beth's comments. She looked as happy as when she proudly performed her striptease. Lisa's intuition, and not her common sense, was right on. I knew each one of us had a great deal to say on every point of her outburst and her honest speech. Yet I remained silent for a while, aware that I had lost objectivity.

Thinking about what Lisa said, I was concerned with the "business" of feeling *normal.*

How does one know what it's like to feel normal, I wondered, knowing that one is capable of feeling only one's own sensations, not someone else's?

Would Lisa feel guilty for enhancing what she considers to be her sex toys?

Would changing her body later become a representation of the religious idea of "sin"?

Was Lisa's feeling of satisfaction a temporary state, balancing on the precipice of the next fashion demand of her generation?

Would she realize that bigger breasts do not solve the relationship issues of intimacy?

Was she aware of the health issues regarding implants being "recalled"? The medical syndromes?

Was it my role to advise her? Of course not. My mind was racing.

What does it mean, changing and manipulating one's breast size and shape?

What emotions does it attempt to cover up? Shame? Doubt?

Can we be rid of shame and doubt by changing the form of the female body?

More than two million women have made this body modification. Do they experience less shame? Or do they now have to deal with shame and guilt?

Is it possible to feel normal in our breast-obsessed world?

"Grace," I said, changing the subject and assuming whatever authority I had lost over my group. "Grace, you wanted to share something with us."

Grace squirmed uncomfortably. "It can wait. It's not as urgent as others' issues." I decided to let her be for now. Grace was actually saying that her opinion was not as important as the others'. I'd known that about her for a while. Usually, I would have used such a statement to start a great therapeutic momentum, but at this moment, she could've been right. Moreover, as Grace was answering, I perceived intense body language coming from Rosie. I caught Rosie quietly crying. Still looking at Lisa and Grace, I said, "What is it, Rosie?" That startled her.

"How did you know?" She asked.

"I don't really know. I've just seen you reacting."

Rosie took a deep breath. "I'm not sure how to react. I'm very upset, but it's not about Lisa. I adore you, Lisa, and I admire your guts—but not your judgment! Ever since we started our group, you know how my sister Gail has been living through my experiences. Well, here is another instance when she should have been here, not me. Gail would want the implants for Lisa. Gail has been talking about it constantly. She wants them done so badly. Gail looks like Lisa in so many ways. You know what I mean."

Indeed, we had been hearing a great deal about sister Gail's wishes, her sexuality, her loves, her feelings, her life. Lisa had provided a psychological bridge to Rosie's emotions about her sister.

This gave me a good opening. I got up and walked toward Rosie, feeling a great surge of energy. Rosie looked at me with an expression that asked, "What have I done now?" I motioned her to get up and gave her a reassuring look that I hoped indicated she had done plenty.

I asked Rosie to roll her chair close to Lisa and sit facing her. Then I asked Lisa to cooperate as I worked with Rosie. We knew that Rosie believed her sister Gail was the epitome of femininity and attractiveness. None of us had ever met her nor seen her picture. We were also aware that Rosie did not feel loved, yet she viewed her sister as popular, sexy, lovable, and happy.

Rosie looked at me with some apprehension. But she moved her chair and sat facing Lisa.

"What do you feel?" I started.

"Fine," she answered too fast.

"No," I started again. "Not how do you feel, but rather what do you feel?"

"I told you. I'm upset."

"This is an exercise. Please, turn to Lisa and role-play Gail. Tell Lisa whatever Gail would have felt and said about all this."

The room was quiet. Grace was nodding her head, yes, yes. Pat was on the edge of her seat, smiling. The rest of the group looked interested.

"My sister?" Rosie repeated slowly. "Well, I am assuming."

"Don't assume, honey. You know the text too well," Pat said, leaning forward.

Tina, sitting next to Pat, showed no emotion but lightly touched her shoulder and said softly, "Let her work now. Don't push."

Rosie gained some energy and started. "Look, Lisa, my sister Rosie has been telling me about you. How good-looking you are, how you're full of life and sexiness. Rosie has been talking about you nonstop. Actually, I'm glad I have this opportunity to skip the messenger between us. Rosie is having a hard time in this group. She told me so…"

Rosie stopped the exercise in mid-sentence. Her words were still hanging in the air as she raised her eyes and gazed at me. The question on her face was clear: "Am I doing it right? Is this what I'm supposed to do?" I nodded: "Yes!" Angela, who was intuitive, had figured out Rosie's internal struggle and whispered to her: "You go girl, you're doing great!" Rosie looked back at me and I nodded again. Surprisingly, she went back to the role-play routine and picked up in the exact place she had stopped.

"My sister Rosie, you know, has been like that ever since we were very small. The presence of energetic beautiful women is intimidating to her. We have a cousin who looks like you, Lisa. Rosie did not like to have her over at all. She feels ugly or something and we cannot talk about it. I think I know you well. For a long time now I've heard how you look and how it's so important for you to feel more feminine and sexy. I think I know and understand the need for bigger breasts, to appear as sexy as you can. I envy you, too. All this feminine stuff that women do is so important to me. My sister Rosie doesn't tell you half of how she envies you. I wish she had whatever it takes to act on what she needs to do in this life. I wish I had a really feminine and normal body. I don't want to be ashamed of myself anymore."

She stopped talking and began sobbing hard and loud. A cry from her core was shaking her body. Obviously, Rosie was crying about herself, not her sister. She continued crying for what seemed like a long time. Her navy blue T-shirt was wet with sweat. This was the hardest emotional work the group had ever seen her do.

The women looked at me as if to say, "Is she all right?" I looked around at these familiar faces. Of course she was all right; better than ever, I said to myself. Out loud I said softly, "Rosie, go on. Speak to Lisa for yourself. Let's leave Gail out of it for now. Tell Lisa about yourself." Her crying grew louder and more intense. Grace wanted to get out of her chair and comfort Rosie. I knew her intentions were good, but it was too soon. The work had just begun; I motioned Grace to keep her seat.

Rosie, still crying, began to speak. "This is so hard for me. Lisa, I feel like you are Gail. And now that you are so perfect with your new looks, I feel so insignificant next to you. I get a strange feeling like I'm paralyzed in your presence. You represent all of what I want. I feel a complete failure inside. I don't feel pretty. Guys don't ask me out. I don't feel loved at all. I don't make a difference in anyone's life. I hate my body," and she prodded at the rolls of fat that encased her as if they were armor. "And I hate my face, too. I look like a boy next to you. I wish I were a real normal girl. I wish I had done what you did. No one ever wanted me. There was room for only one girl in our family, and Gail *was* and *is* it. I was supposed to be the boy my parents never had. I hate my life. I have no life. I'm so envious, it's burning me up inside! And I hate that feeling, too. I hate being so envious and so bitter about everything. I think that I've become mean. And I hate that." When she was finished speaking, the room was quiet.

Rosie wiped her red nose and sat thinking for a long while. Finally she said, "What did I just say? I've told you about my real feelings and how I hate myself for having them in the first place.

Does that make sense to anyone?" She stopped and looked around. "I'm done." Catching Lisa's eye, she whispered, "Thank you."

Lisa extended her hands to Rosie and they both embraced. Jane also put her arms around Rosie.

After a long silence, Rosie spoke again. This time her voice sounded like another person was speaking from her throat. She sighed out loud and said, "Gee, what a lift! I feel so different. I needed that."

I've known these women for some time now, and trusted myself with a decision to continue the process for a while longer. I looked straight into Grace's eyes. I had noticed in the past that Grace, in spite of her low self-image and tendency to belittle herself, did occasionally rebel. This time she did. Her gaze was steady as she looked into my eyes.

Finally Grace began speaking. "I have a couple of strong reactions to Lisa's, um, dramatic announcement." She paused, and then said, "First, I don't get it. The need to invade one's body with foreign substances worries me. Second, your ability, Lisa, to make a major decision that may be irreversible is beyond me. And third, you have now awakened the eye of the storm in my life."

She spoke slowly and painfully. Grace did not expose her private life easily. Her parents had immigrated to California from Toronto, Canada, when she was fourteen years old, and they continued to refer to Toronto as their home. She prides herself on the modest life that she has, often avoiding the frantic pace that many of her friends and neighbors live. Now sixty-four years old, she was retired from a social work career that she'd pursued for twenty-six years. Usually very resourceful, she often brought outstanding research articles that she'd come across in her readings to share in our group process.

Grace's family remained the center of her universe. Her two sons were professionals who married professional women. The third child was a daughter who had been married to a musician for two years. Grace often talked about this youngest child of hers.

"Remember how I was concerned about Amy? Well, she has been on my mind day and night lately. Amy and her husband Josh make a sweet young couple, and I think she is lucky to have Josh as a mate for life. But they hardly ever talk about starting a family. I assumed it was because Josh, being a musician, was not ready. Well, I found out that it's much more complicated than that—complicated and messy." She stopped for air. Jane passed her a tissue. Everyone sat patiently waiting for her to continue.

"I found out that Amy and Josh had this huge fight. Apparently, Josh is the one who wants children soon. He wants to participate in raising them, you know, like so many young fathers today. He actually wants to be an equal caretaker since he is home most days. He finally sat Amy down and they really talked it through. Josh found out from Amy that she had made a decision never to breast-feed her babies. She does not want her breasts to be ruined. She wants them to be perky forever, she said. I'd never known this about her. Josh is so beside himself. He cannot believe that his own kids will not be breast-fed. He is into health foods, yoga, mental health, you know. During their fight—which is what it became—they mentioned getting a divorce." She paused and looked around at the rest of us.

"I'm dying inside. And now to come here and see this." Grace pointedly looked at Lisa. "Another one with breasts on her brains. Don't you know what they are made for? What has gotten into you all?" She shot us an exasperated look. "I wish to protest this so-called progress. I think you are all nuts. Your breasts were put on earth for the purpose of breast-feeding not breast-dancing or breast-parading. Breasts no matter how they look *are normal!* They're not status symbols. They're not just there to tell the difference between men and women. They're a genetic disposition." She looked aghast, then pulled herself together and added, "I don't believe what just came out of my mouth."

"You just wanted to share that, didn't you?" Pat asked quietly.

"Yes, but I feel awful about sharing. Look what I have done," Grace said, looking around at our faces, some of which registered surprise, others amusement. "Maybe I should have kept it to myself."

I did not participate in making Grace feel better. She represented an interesting contradiction. On the one hand, she was knowledgeable and educated, well-read and experienced. On the other hand, she sometimes sounded as though she was clueless about what was actually going on. It was especially true about her relationships with those people dearest to her, much like the shoemaker's children who went barefoot because their father was so busy at his trade that he didn't have time to make them shoes.

"What do we have here?" I asked the room.

Tina, who up until now had remained quiet, blurted out, "We have two brand new boobs, two worried mamas, and endless envious females all in one group."

Isabel smiled, "Yes, I'm burning too. I want a perfect body. I could use some improvement, though it's not urgent. I'm jealous, so sue me." Her words were accompanied by increasingly wild hand gestures, while her body danced in her chair. Some of us laughed, including me.

Angela said wistfully, "You've read my mind; I'd always wished my body was closer to perfect."

"Now, what do we really have here?" I asked.

"I'm not shocked," said Katherine, "but I realize some pretty serious things about us. You, Lisa, moved me. I also liked your process, Rosie. It's just so hard for me to hear Angela. Well, I shouldn't say that, Ange. You have the right to your feelings. I just wish I could relax with my imperfect body. It will never meet the beauty standards of any of you. I have to live *in* it and *with* it. There is no limit to beauty and sex appeal. Angela to me is a rare external beauty. That was before I knew her inner world. Are we all so enslaved to others' standards? Will someone as beautiful as

Angela ever be just content? Are we cursed with ending each day feeling diminished?"

I repeated Katherine's questions about feeling content with our bodies or feeling diminished at the end of the day. "Let me ask you this, did any of your *mothers* ever feel what Katherine has suggested?" I questioned. Each one looked around the room.

"The answer is a big nope! Since no one answered." Jane said.

"We've sure done a fine job in our generation, reducing ourselves to a collection of separate body parts," Grace said annoyingly.

"You meant tits and ass," Tina said.

"Before you get carried away by the body parts police," I said, bringing back a subject that had been passed over, "have you noticed that most of us have lots of different feelings about the feelings we originally had regarding an issue?"

Rosie looked like she was afraid of what was coming. She felt she'd said enough for now.

Lisa gave me a sideways glance, half-interested. She wanted to talk about looking feminine, since she figured she held the tickets to that show. She also had a date lined up for later that night.

Jane said, "What was that?" Others prodded me to answer the question I had just posed.

Beth came to the rescue. She had easily understood this psychological concept and, as in the past, had been a tremendous support to the group. Beth repeated the question, "Dr. Nili asked us, 'Have we noticed that most of us have lots of different feelings about the feelings we originally had regarding an issue?'" They heard this time, and I realized that the concept was new to some.

"Want some examples?" I asked. They did.

"Let's see. We had Lisa today, sharing blissfully, and minutes later explaining away the feelings of aliveness and joy. Almost apologizing for feeling so alive." Lisa started to jump in with yet another explanation, but I told her to wait. "Then we had Beth, showing strong anger that turned into regret for raining on the parade, so to speak. Later we watched Rosie who has intense feelings about her life and hating herself for having her feelings about the feelings." Rosie looked like she was about to protest. "Yes, Rosie," I continued, "you make plenty of sense. Last but not least, we had Grace who has been trying for a few weeks to tell us her feelings about her daughter, Amy. She was feeling so badly about her own feelings that she waited until Lisa provoked her. Now she feels shame and doubt about her own precious feelings.

"We are entitled to our feelings," I said. "Whatever they are. Guess what? We are even entitled to ambivalent feelings. Those are the ones we have daily. Namely, two different or opposite emotions about the same issue.

"When we have feelings about our feelings, the original subject of concern will not be dealt with. Those feelings about the feelings are intense, and they will surface first. You may detect them in our attitudes, tone, and body language. Those feelings take up a great deal of our emotional energy."

"This is so much to think about," Beth said.

"Yes," said Tina, "that is enough to think about for today. But I still want to talk more about Lisa's new breasts."

"It's interesting you mentioned that, Tina," I said. "I'd like to take the opportunity now to bring you back to focus." I looked at each of them. "I want to try something with you." I leaned in closer, looking at each woman until I was sure I had her attention. "I want you to turn your chairs around, facing away from each other." They were used to my exercises and did so, although some reluctantly.

"Now," I said, "I want you to close your eyes. Relax. Clear your head of everything and let my voice penetrate your subconscious." I had gradually lowered and softened my voice. This is the voice I'd trained myself especially for hypnoisis. "I want to put you in a setting—a peaceful, tranquil setting that is safe. Now take a deep breath and gradually let it out." They did so, and I could see many of them relaxing.

"You are at a good friend's country place. It is just the two of you. Her lovely house is surrounded by lush woods, all of which is surrounded by a high fence. You are totally secluded. No one else is within miles of you.

"You've been writing in your journal while your friend is taking a nap. You decide to take a break and leave her a note that you are going for a walk in the peaceful woods. You put on your hiking boots and stuff your journal and a bottle of water in your backpack. When you set out, it's late afternoon. The sun is shining. There's not a cloud in the sky. A light breeze caresses your face. You walk along well-marked paths, through firs and birch trees, all of them sparkling in the sun.

"After about an hour, you come to a clearing. You're warm now, and you take out the water and drink. Looking around, you can see, through a break in the trees, the setting sun glimmering off the water of a small lake. You walk toward it and watch the placid, still water, which is so clear and calm that you can see yourself in it. You take off your boots and socks and roll up your trousers. When you wade into the water, you're surprised at how warm it is. You smile and decide to go for a dip. You take off your clothes and carefully lay them on the rocks."

At this point Lisa giggled. "Lisa," I admonished. I quickly looked around at the others who all had their eyes closed. Most looked relaxed, and some were smiling. Rosie, however, was quietly weeping, the tears falling down her cheeks.

"You take off your clothes," I continued, and I saw Pat start up.

"I can't," she said with quiet determination.

I paused. "All right, Pat," I said. "You can walk into the water, which is perfectly safe," I assured her, "and then you can take off your clothes. I'll take them and lay them out on a rock to dry." I watched her carefully, and she reluctantly nodded.

"Now, wade into the lake slowly," I continued. The sun is setting, so there is very little light—just enough so you can see that you are safe. The lake is shallow. The water comes up to your shoulders and no more, even at the deepest part. So you wade slowly into the water until it has reached your shoulders. This is a weekend for recreation—for *re*-creation," I emphasized. "Here is a moment your spiritual aspect may surface. Try to feel that side of you.

"Bring your arms to the water's surface. Lift up one hand, then the other. Now drop your arms under the water and raise your hands, one at a time. See how they float easily to the surface? How easy it is to move them?

"Now cup your breasts, placing your right hand on your right breast, your left on the left one. You feel that they are different, aren't they? In weight, in size, in shape. They are amorphous as if they had lost their shape, as if they had lost their identity. Now step back until you have freed your breasts from the water. They have definition again, don't they? They are your own familiar breasts.

"Step farther into the water so they are submerged again. Cup them in your hands again. In your mind's eye look around at the beauty of your setting. Take it all in. Now close your eyes again and feel how you are one with this beauty, with the still, clear lake, the tall, handsome trees, and their leaves softly rustling and murmuring in the breeze.

"Release your breasts and let them float free. Now, cup them again, only this time place your right hand on your left breast and your left hand on your right breast. Continue to listen and remember your reactions.

"Many women have told me that they have fantasized about what their ideal breasts would look like—ideal in terms of size, shape, color, and texture. Now imagine your ideal breasts. What would they be like? Their texture? Their feel? Their weight? Their shape? Their size? What color are your nipples? Are your breasts similar to your imagined picture of your ideal breasts? Are they identical? Somewhat? Not at all? Or did you never have an ideal breast in mind?

"Now take a deep breath and relax. What emotions have been raised?

"Are you sad? Disappointed? Joyful? Appreciative?

"Do you feel forgotten by God or forgotten by Mother Nature?

"Would you be willing to share your feelings with another person?

"If your ideal breasts are different from your own, where did you get your idea of ideal breasts from? From another woman? Your mother? Society?

"If your own breasts are not what you consider ideal, are you willing to live with them for the rest of your life?

"What feelings does this exercise provoke in you?"

I paused. "We're going to get out of the water soon. Take your hands away and look at your breasts floating there. Really look at them. Now, even if you don't like them, give them an affirmation for not betraying you so far. Then slowly step out of the water. Pat, here are your clothes. It's now totally dark. As you step out, feel the water subsiding, from your shoulders, your breasts, your hips, your thighs.

"After you are dressed, take your journal out of the backpack and sit on the rocks. Watch the moon rise above the still lake. Listen to the murmur of the trees. And in the light of the full moon, write down what you have just experienced."

I let them settle down and come out of their experience. "You can turn your chairs around now," I said. They did so and were quiet for several minutes. Most of the women were writing in their journals, which we keep locked in the office.

As we got up to leave, Tina asked, "May I try this at home?" Everyone laughed.

That evening I got home early. My conversation with myself had started in the car as I asked, "My mom would have never doubted her femininity, would she?" I had a hard time with that. No, my mom would not have, I concluded, and sighed with relief. This is a generational thing with us, I thought. In this generation there are "degrees" to the concept of femininity. The women in my groups and seminars are preoccupied with doubts about the quality and extent of their femininity.

The streetlight changed as I approached the last intersection near my home. I pushed the gas pedal down some more, almost pushing myself. Would I doubt my femininity? "Come on," I said to myself, "you self-righteous therapist, show some honesty, please." Yes, I'm somewhat envious at some women's perfect bodies. I parked the car and was aware of the aftertaste of having feelings about my feelings.

I indulged in some very interesting readings that evening. Over the years, I have developed a passion for books. I like to read them, of course, and I also like to look at them, touch them, and sometimes smell them. This is not a fetish. My grandfather was a bookbinder, but not just ordinary books—leather-covered ones with fourteen-carat gold detailed decoration embedded around the covers. Major organizations and some prominent people had his handmade ordered book covers for special occasions. He had turned the bookbinding craft into an art. I loved to sit and watch him labor over each detail. My grandmother Sarah worked along with him. She was energetic and full of life. He was slow and thoughtful. A pair made in heaven, I thought. Their workshop was above their home on the second floor. My grandparents' home had always smelled of leather, glue, and paper. I loved that scent. Books were always present as far in the past as my memory can serve me.

Reading sounded like the perfect anesthetic to my overly stimulated mind. Or so I thought. Alas, the book I selected on narcissism was too difficult to concentrate on so late at night.

Several years ago, I had read this book about a narcissistic patient. While the language of the book is English, the dialect is psychoanalytic literature. In his book *Shame: The Underside of Narcissism,* Andrew P. Morrison suggests:

> Several related feelings often reflect shame experiences, for example embarrassment, remorse, mortification, apathy, and lowered self esteem. However, because of the intensity of its pain, shame, in the clinical encounter, may be concealed and hidden from oneself or the therapist.

Later in the book, Morrison explains how strong emotions such as anger, rage, contempt, and envy may represent an attempt to deal with the intolerable shame. He emphasizes the role shame frequently plays in generating ridicule, defiance, and boredom.

As the evening wore on, I read aloud as if Lisa, Angela, Tina, and Rosie were in my living room. I read for us regarding Morrison's ideas on the presence of shame as intolerable.

> The self may thus attempt to purge shame through attacks on objects, living or inanimate, that momentarily can be seen as shame's source.

Morrison was describing Lisa's behaviors quite accurately. Lisa had been very uncomfortable with her body. She used to tell us in group meetings the upsetting feelings she'd have while dating. Not long ago she was in love with a young man, but could not bring herself to engage in touching and fondling with him. She was ashamed of the way her body looked. She used to feel that her body was underdeveloped and that she could never be proud of it. At times, she sounded as if she was obsessed with the smallness of her breasts.

Lisa had chosen her breasts as her "source of shame." They were the objects she attacked in an attempt to get rid of the shame.

Would her new, improved breasts take care of the feeling "not good enough?"

Was this solution temporary, since her breasts were a symbol for something else?

And Rosie's rage. She still felt injured and attacked her external looks, disregarding and degrading herself and "using" her sister Gail, Lisa, and her cousin in her narcissistic rage.

Would I bring this information to the group?

Would I show them the traditional clinical interpretations of my observations?

Would I create more shame when I exposed our need for perfection as mere "narcissistic rage"?

In case psychoanalytic explanations are a bit too much, here is an eyewitness account from the physician in the delivery room, as described in Dr. Northrup's *Women's Bodies, Women's Wisdom.*

> I have been in the delivery room countless times when a female baby is born and the woman who had just given birth looks up at her husband and says, 'Honey, I am sorry'—apologizing because the baby is not a son! The self-rejection of the mother herself, apologizing for the product of her own nine-month gestation period, labor and delivery, is staggering to experience.

Looking back at the moment of birth of my first son, I realized then that the expressions of joy were natural. I do honestly recall, however, a sense of relief that I had not just done something good but very good. Over thirty years ago, I had bought into the cultural persuasiveness on gender issues in our lives.

Having accepted cultural perceptions is one thing. But having feelings about those feelings is another.

Chapter Three

BREASTOLOGY *101*

The Following Week

What to do with breasts, if one is not actually using them, has preoccupied the feminine mind for a very long time.

—from *Femininity,* by Susan Brownmiller

If we think about how women's genitals are physically concealed, unlike men's and how women's breasts are physically exposed, unlike men's, it can be seen differently: women's breasts, then correspond to men's penises as the vulnerable 'sexual flower' on the body, so that to display the former and conceal the latter makes women's bodies vulnerable while men's are protected.

—from *The Beauty Myth,* by Naomi Wolf

A T THE BEGINNING OF EACH MEETING, WE PRACTICE A ROUTINE that lasts ten to fifteen minutes and melts the ice between the reality outside the group and the actual process. This exercise put us in touch with what is happening with the group members in the present moment, like taking one's body temperature. Within minutes, we are updated about what has transpired and what unresolved issues there might be from the last meeting. I learned this routine from my great seminar teacher, Dr. Lori Gordon. In her book *Passages to Intimacy,* Dr. Gordon describes this learning tool. She calls it Daily Temperature Reading:

> Confiding—the ability to reveal yourself fully, honestly and directly to another human being—is the lifeblood of intimacy. It's frightening to be in a close relationship in which silences, hidden agendas, contradictions and inconsistencies are a steady diet.

Since I had been trained by Dr. Gordon to lead P.A.I.R.S. programs for individuals seeking higher quality skills for their relationships, I adopted the Daily Temperature Reading exercise to jump-start most of our group meetings.

This exercise, which is one of numerous tools for intimate relationships, is part of the program called P.A.I.R.S., or Practical Applications of Intimate Relationship Skills. Dr. Gordon had created the P.A.I.R.S. programs over two decades ago and it has been taught throughout the world. In this effective procedure, the participants "volunteer" information in five structured steps.

Step one is **Appreciation.** People need to be recognized and validated by those who are intimately close to them. In our tight group, a few appreciations were expressed at this session.

"I would like to appreciate you, Rosie, for opening yourself up so profoundly last week," said Pat at the beginning of our session.

Beth was the second one to speak. "I would like to appreciate you, Dr. Nili, whose therapeutic cage was rattled when Lisa undressed in the middle of a group meeting. Most of the women here don't know how difficult it is for a therapist to be tested like that. My appreciation to you for not losing your cool."

Step two is **New Information.** "Intimacy thrives only when partners know what is happening in each other's lives," writes Dr. Gordon.

"I'd like to distribute some copies I made for our home reading," said Grace. The material relates to one of the sessions in the recent past. I would like to discuss it next week." She handed out copies of recent popular psychology articles she had photocopied. The group treasured the fresh information she shared.

New information also includes personal data. Isabel said, "I will not be here next week. I need to take some time for some medical tests, and I don't want to discuss it yet. I'll miss you all," she added and smiled, "and I promise not to make major decisions about my life without discussing them first with you."

Katherine announced that she had met a man who was interested in seeing her, and she was surprised that she was equally interested in seeing him. "For now, though," she said, "it's too soon to talk about it."

Step three is **Puzzles.** These include clarifications and explanations of any subjects that remain unclear from last time.

Rosie said to Isabel, "I know about the tests. Tell us about the results." Isabel demurred.

Step four is **Complaints with a Request for Change.** Without blame or demand, a group member may state the behavior she wishes to correct.

Today, Lisa said, "If there is a next time, I should not be made to feel so guilty for showing a part of my body to my best friends."

Isabel contributed, "I would like to make sure we are invited to share about major life decisions with the group. Also, the group will be supportive at all times."

Step five is sharing **Hopes, Wishes, and Dreams.** This step gives us a chance to reflect on what we want for ourselves in the future.

Tina said, "To those of us who wish for them, I hope and dream of these beautiful boobs we have witnessed."

"Amen," said Rosie.

"Thanks," Lisa said laughingly.

"Any leftovers from last time?" I asked.

Beth wanted to start. "I've been thinking about you, Lisa. I've never given any importance to my own breasts, as you seem to do. I'm definitely from a different era than you. I could easily be your mother. I see lots of people in our community work. Often I hear women talking about their imperfect bodies. My body is imperfect for modeling swimsuits. I see that. Lisa, you'll have a wonderful career and life, and I care about you. I want you to look at me, at my aging body, which I carry with great respect." She then turned to include Rosie. "Rosie, Lisa, I'm forty-eight years old. My body is fine for its own lifeline. Also, I don't use my body as a tool in my career. Like Grace and Dr. Nili, I mostly use my listening skills and experiences in the mental health field to make an impact in my daily work. My body doesn't participate much. So, I guess I'm telling you that, for its purpose in my career, my body as it is now is precisely what I need. I enjoy it and I feel loved.

"I've also been thinking about your Amy, Grace. You're right. She does belong to another generation that lost the message. I mean, our breasts were made for breast-feeding. They're not really about our looks, are they?"

Beth stopped for a second and looked around. "I don't want to imply self love. I want to appreciate your openness and to say that you are on my mind many hours each week." She paused. "Actually, the subject of love of self is not such a bad idea."

Angela spoke before Beth had a chance to continue that thought. "Thanks, Beth, for reminding me. But I have almost the same occupation as Lisa—and the same concerns. Lisa's acting and my modeling professions are merciless careers. I understand Lisa too well. I'm not worried about her. She has done the right thing and at the right time for her." Turning to Grace, she added, "I had no chance to consider breast-feeding and the reason the two are mutually exclusive. I think a woman can have it all today."

Angela stopped and looked back at Lisa. "I guess I'm finished talking for you for today." Angela lowered her head for a moment, and when she raised it, we realized she was crying. This was very unusual for her. The group was silent.

Angela looked at Beth and took a deep breath. "I know how careful you are with us. I personally wish I had you for a mom. I don't feel loved. I did not feel loved in my past, and I still don't feel it now. I mean, I don't feel it from my husband. *I believe* the words I hear from you, but I cannot identify with them. I had no intention of feeling sorry for myself, but I must admit I'm feeling that now."

She was silent again, and no one interrupted her. Finally, I said, "Angela, could you give yourself permission to focus with us on that pain?" She looked up, nodded, and then hugged her long, slim arms around herself, put her head down on her chest, and started to weep again.

"Give it a voice," I said, motioning to Grace, who was about to embrace Angela, to remain seated.

Angela cried, "I don't feel loved. It's not working for me and I hate my life." Then softly she said, "It's not fair, it's not fair, it's not fair." Her litany intensified and she screamed out, "It's not fair! It's not fair!" She was now crying uncontrollably.

We sat quietly for a few minutes. Some bowed their heads, not in shame at Angela's outburst, but simply to give her some emotional space. Others smiled lovingly at her, and there were tears in some of their eyes. In a few minutes, Angela's crying subsided, and she thanked us for being supportive. She was smiling now. She looked more beautiful than ever; Lisa even commented on it. Beth explained that being vulnerable does this to us—something to do with inner beauty. We all agreed.

Obviously, the pain Angela had held in for so long had surfaced. Her declaration that she felt better was true but temporary.

"I want you to talk about the unfairness you see in your life," I said. "Right now if you wish."

"No," Angela answered quickly. "I'll take you on at another time. Thanks."

"All right," I said. "We can wait." I turned to Grace, who knows how to find information of significant educational value, something she justifiably takes pride in.

Her assignment for today was from *Dr. Susan Love's Breast Book* and she read an excerpt from it. It was almost as if, after a particularly cathartic part of a church service, we now turned to the next reading of the lesson.

> Most women don't know what 'normal' breasts look like. Most of us haven't seen many other women's breasts, and have been constantly exposed since childhood to the 'ideal' image of breasts that permeated our society. But few of us fit that image, and there's no reason why we should. The range of size and shape of breasts is so wide that it's hard to say what's 'normal.' Not only are there very large and very small breasts, but also in most women one breast is slightly larger than the other. Breast size is genetically determined; it depends chiefly on the percentage of fat to other tissue in the breasts. Usually about a third of the breast is composed of fat tissue. The rest is breast tissue. The fat can vary as you gain or lose weight; the breast tissue remains constant.

The women were paying close attention as Grace continued to read.

> Breast size has nothing to do with capacity to make milk, or with vulnerability to cancer or other breast disease. Very large breasts, however, can be physically uncomfortable, and, like very small or uneven breasts, they can be emotionally uncomfortable as well. Often there is a ridge of fat at the bottom of the breast. This 'infra-mammary

ridge' is normal, the result of our breasts folding over themselves because we walk upright. Many women find that their nipples don't face front; they stick out slightly toward the armpit. There's a reason for this. Picture yourself holding the baby you are about to nurse. The baby's head is held in the crook of your arm—a nipple pointing to the side is comfortably close to the baby's mouth.

Suddenly, there were hands in the air, like students in a class. How typical this is to the psychology of groups: If you behave toward them as a teacher, they'll become a class of students. They were educated and entertained. Lisa did not know about the "side kick," as she called it. Tina and Isabel admitted this was news to them, too.

Grace put away her text and added, "You know, this is so true for me. That is why I bought into this myth. As a young woman, I'd never seen breasts, like, you know what I mean, several women together. I don't mean sexually." She shot an admonishing look to Lisa, who was about to say something. "I was brought up quite protected by conservative parents. No summer camps, no slumber parties. I had to be self-educated. The sixties sure helped me find out what goes in where. Finally, I learned to have sex and it took the rest of my life to learn to make love. I was curious about what was normal. I wish that, back then, I had seen just the sight of a few women in the nude. Imagine that."

"You mean like in a painting by Rubens?" Jane suggested.

"Who's Rubens?" Lisa asked.

Ignoring Lisa's lack of knowledge of art history, Tina made an appreciative comment about Grace's education. She also didn't know how common it was for the size of each breast to vary. She asked if anyone else was aware of it.

"Tina," Pat said, "I have a good example of how sizes vary. I'd never known it to be true until now. I thought it was just my mother and me. What a relief!" She began to cry quietly. "It's so hard to speak about it," she said when she had gotten under control. "My mom and I were so close. She died, as you know, of breast cancer. I guess I am so afraid for my own life, you know. When I heard about the normality of having one breast bigger, I cannot help myself. Sorry. I was thinking that I'm like my mom who had one breast bigger than the other. So I thought that it was a sign I might get cancer too. My mom used to refer to her breasts' asymmetry as an abnormality. She used to say that this might be why she got sick. The bigger breast got the cancer first, then the smaller one. No one ever said anything about the normalcy of size variation."

After a brief silence, Katherine said, "I'm so mad at some physicians. This is bordering on neglect. Pat, honey, I'm so sorry that they did not inform you and save you and your mom months of worrying. I also have one breast bigger than the other one. I wish I'd known you a few years back when you were struggling with differentiating between mom and self. This is not a health hazard."

"Just being a woman is dangerous," Pat said, almost in a whisper. The others laughed, even though they knew she meant it seriously.

Katherine rolled in her chair backward. She was shuffling in her bag making noise. "Sorry about that," she started talking as she pulled up a white and green book from her disheveled-looking leather bag. "I can't help it. I'm now reading this fascinating book for women. I had wanted to share it with you as soon as I was finished reading it. However, Pat's last remark about being a woman is dangerous; I need to share it now, even though I'm not finished reading it." As she was talking, Katherine was flipping through the pages of *Natural Hormone Balance for Women* by Uzzi Reiss, M.D. Finally, she found the place in the book she intended to show us next week, took a deep breath, and read:

> A woman's shape and breast size during her younger years serve as a superb yardstick of estrogen production. These details suggest how much of the hormone she may need in a replacement program.

For this purpose, we use three categories of body types. Type one and two experience very different physiological responses to high or low estrogen.

Estrogen Type One: Short, Voluptuous, and Full-Breasted. This woman produces more estrogen. She functions on a relatively higher level. The abundance of estrogen creates larger breasts, earlier bone closure, and smaller stature.

Estrogen Type Two: Taller, Thinner, and Relatively Small-Breasted. Here, the woman operates on much less estrogen and usually develops her period later. She has grown taller because of less estrogen in the system to promote the calcification of bone tissue. Smaller breast size is a sign of relatively lower estrogen.

Estrogen Type Three: "In-betweeners". Here we find the largest number of women. They produce an average amount of estrogen, with some tending toward the high end and others toward the low end."

Katherine put the book down and seemed to be looking at Lisa. "This estrogen is a mystery. Does anyone need help to modify the medical language?"

Three hands went up in the air and again, Katherine generously explained the correlation between breast size and amounts of estrogen production in a woman's body. She had succeeded in making it sound very matter of fact, with her voice calm and her mannerisms empathetic.

Now our group had shifted the focus to the role of hormones and breast size. For one moment in the history of this group, I felt that the burden of the "breast size issue" was lifted. But that moment was short lived as Rosie announced that she felt unlucky because she didn't get enough estrogen.

At this point Beth remembered a paragraph she read to us few months ago, quoting from *Survival of the Prettiest* by Nancy Etcoff, Ph.D. I looked for it in my drawer and read:

> Female breasts are like no others in the mammalian world. Human females are the only mammals who develop rounded breasts at puberty and keep them whether or not they are producing milk. Other mammals have breasts that swell only when they are full of milk, collapsing when breast feeding is over. Breasts are not sex symbols to other mammals, anything but, since they indicate a pregnant or lactating and infertile female. To chimps, gorillas, and orangutans, breasts are sexual turnoffs.

My group therapy had taken a turn and become a sincere study group. "I recall showing this paragraph to my son Edan one day," I said. They all looked at me expectantly. "I was going over some of this information when he was visiting me, and he asked me what I was studying. I told him, and my college graduate replied, "So now, Mom, you're teaching Breastology 101?" This got them laughing again, but I sensed Pat wanted to say more.

She cleared her throat, now feeling supported by the group and prepared to go out on a limb. She looked at Katherine, then at me, and finally, giggling, asked the group, "Have any of you ever seen other women's breasts—in the nude, I mean, excluding sisters, mothers, and daughters?"

"What a terrific question! Good for you," Beth said. I was sure that the reply would be positive for all of the others, and I waited eagerly for the enthusiastic answers to come. Surely they've all seen other women naked in their health clubs, at the very least.

"How did you feel about it?" I asked.

Katherine, of course, had seen an abundance of breasts in her medical training, but the group did not accept that as natural. They admitted, however, that Katherine's perspective would be invaluable concerning what was "normal." And Katherine confirmed that her clinical experiences, while sobering, did not involve intimate or personal experiences.

"In my training," she said, "I've seen a great deal of pathology. It's not like one's personal life. First, I had learned to detach myself. I've seen lots of breasts, women's and young girls'. Would you believe I've seen men with breast problems? What I've seen and studied had nothing to do with women's nudity though. It was, however, about pathology, abnormalities, and disease. I've become so desensitized. I've developed a deep appreciation for prevention. I'm excited about healthy bodies. I'll talk about prevention any time. But I shouldn't respond to this question. Has anyone else seen naked, real ones?"

"Wait," I said, not wishing to miss this boat. "You're missing the best question here. It's not if you've seen breasts. I'm sure you have. The main question here is what were your reactions to the sight of your first realistic, unfamiliar, naked breasts? How old were you? Where were you? What happened? Katherine's answer began to describe it, but she went 'medical' on us. Anyone else on first reaction?"

Jane, Grace, and Pat had not seen nude women at an early age. Beth had run summer camps for many years and had seen many girls changing after swimming. "It all seemed familiar," she said. "I must have been in camps like that myself. I don't recall a reaction to their breasts. I noticed, however, that the younger generations of girls have much thinner bodies than the girls of my era."

Rosie added, "I've seen others. It was a trauma for me every single time. I considered and still consider my body deformed next to most females. I don't want to see others naked ever again." She paused. "Actually, I don't like this question."

Isabel, who grew up abroad and spent her summers in Nice and other places in the south of France, said, "I've seen a few women on the beach, sunning topless. There were others walking everywhere, showing beautiful erect breasts like there was no gravity!" We laughed. "There is a great freedom about nudity over there. It's not a big deal. Every summer we went on a long vacation and I got my sex education while the rest of the family got a deep tan. Seriously, our summers were a great way to get to know one another again. But back to breasts, I was not surprised by any variations in breasts' size and shape. I've seen them in many sizes—the way they were made."

Lisa mentioned that back in her cheerleader years she had seen many girls naked. "Rosie," she said, "during those days I used to feel so weird. I had the only flat chest in a world hungry for some tits. My parents did not want to hear about it. I had two girlfriends who had some breasts, but we felt the same about our breasts and our fantasy lives. Compared to other girls, we felt unlucky and like rejected."

"Anyone else want to share their impressions of others' breasts at a younger age?" I asked. There was no reply. "Okay, then, I guess I'll share mine." I paused to collect my thoughts. "You should have been there, all of you." I started to smile. They laughed.

"You know how girls serve in the Israeli Army right after high school?"

"Oh God," Grace exploded, laughing, "don't tell me they do it in the Holy Land!"

"Grace!" two or three of the women said, slightly shocked.

"Well," I continued, "this was my very first day in the service. We were told to take showers by certain unit order, meaning one unit at a time for a very limited time. Three decades later I'm still figuring out if this was done to save water."

Jane said, "Don't joke now. This is too good."

"There were twenty-five girls, ages eighteen to twenty, tired— no, exhausted. It was boot camp, after all. They made us run all day, change our uniforms, practice making the beds the army way, obey orders on clearing the tent area, clean our guns. We were so dirty and sweaty that I could not tell who was who. Then we got

an order to hit the showers and get ready for the chief comman-
der's first inspection.

"The words 'first inspection' still echoed in my mind as I ran to
those little huts made of tin called camp showers. We barged in,
pushing each other purposefully. There were five spigots hanging
from the wall without their showerheads. The water was streaming
out like it was coming from an end of a garden hose. How I missed
home on that first day. Then someone said 'first inspection' and we
became soldiers again. Two minutes later, I heard laughter. I
looked up from undoing my dirty army boots and thought I was
hallucinating. Either I was exhausted or had been thrown into the
middle of a gorgeous Rubens painting!"

"Who's *Rubens?*" Lisa pleaded, but was shushed silent by the
others who were laughing.

"There were naked women everywhere. Bodies, breasts, pubic
hair, and butts of every size and shape. The transition from obey-
ing orders and operating like a robot to this greatest discovery on
earth was so very intense that I forgot to function. They were 'in
my face.' So many different shapes and sizes of boobs everywhere.
Most were very erect. Some were very small. A few were as large
as my mother's. All I remember is being shoved and pushed by my
friends in slow motion. I recall the sensation of water on me, the
scent of soap, the feel of these wet bodies and wet hair, and one
big puddle of soapy water on the floor. I heard myself saying 'first
inspection' again and again.

"Years later, I've learned that humans have an innate need to
make sense of stuff, so my repeating 'first inspection' was an attempt
to make the experience of what I was seeing congruent with the
context. After all, it was my first breast show and my first inspection.

"Later that night, I digested the event. I loved the magnificence
of nature. In fact, I was in awe of the tremendous beauty hidden
under the dusty uniforms. Suddenly, however, I became self-conscious—remember Eve in the Garden of Eden? What about my
whole body? Am I part of this creation or am I forgotten? In the

darkness of the huge tent where my friends were sleeping, I remembered touching myself everywhere, like taking inventory. Thank you, God, I was all there."

The group was silent.

Finally, Tina said, "You're right. I wish I had been there."

Rosie looked up and asked in a child's voice, "Do you really think that human bodies are part of the beauty of nature?"

"Rosie," I said slowly, "it's not what I think that will count in the long run. How *you* feel about this body you live in will determine the quality of your life."

It's remarkable how most of these mature, intelligent, productive women who hold such prominence in their respective families, careers, communities, and friendships are ready to doubt their femininity.

I was home folding laundry when I realized that I wasn't focusing on what I was doing. Totally preoccupied with the subject of a woman's need to validate her femininity, I wondered: Is this need for validation for one's femininity true for other women?

Is the fact of women doubting their own femininity a new phenomenon?

Am I feeling these feelings of doubts too?

Is questioning a woman's femininity really about self-worth?

What about the generation before us? Had my mother, or the other women's mothers and their peers, ever displayed such doubt regarding their femininity?

Looking back, I don't recall my mother's friends questioning their identity in quite that way.

Still, I wanted to know what I had missed in my recollections. It was near midnight when I realized I was wide awake and focused on a past generation's perception of femininity. A search in my library did not bring me much satisfaction. Not enough history-oriented books. I thought about checking the university library but immediately canceled that idea. I wanted to ask someone, to interview them. But whom could I approach?

The answer was so simple it completely caught me by surprise. It was past midnight, which made the timing perfect. I picked up the phone and called my own mother in Israel. It was morning there.

"Good morning, Ma," I said, when she picked up the receiver. "It's time for an interview." She laughed and asked me to wait while she let the dog out. I could hear the dog barking and its friendly face came to my mind. When she returned, I asked her to go back four or five decades and give me an account of how it was to feel feminine. Were women preoccupied with sex appeal? Was it an issue? What about breast size? Was it a topic of discussion?

Boy, was she ready for me!

"Look," she said in the voice that I'd missed so much, "we did have concerns about appearances. Looking feminine wasn't difficult. Those were the days before blue jeans. Women always wore dresses. Consider the fact that our lives were a part of a working middle class with no exposure to glamour or rich-and-famous lifestyles. We had a large, active social life. Dieting was not a subject; neither was body size. Breasts were not a preoccupation like in your generation. As a woman, I'd learned to accentuate what we called looking 'chic' and having 'class' in my posture, looks, attitudes, and manners."

She was right. I've seen them, her women friends, over the years. And my mom is, indeed, a classy lady. There was no doubt about that.

"Ma, you were doing things like hair and nails—an external expression of popular beauty and its industry—but what was most important, if you can summarize it for me?"

"Well, yes," she said, "externally being in style and attractive was pretty important. I remember how making our clothes, more than shopping for them, made us feel so good about ourselves."

I thought about that. Damn the phone! I wished I could have seen her face. What she said next was music to my ears. "Having babies was the way you expressed your feminine potential. It goes without saying that the pursuit of that goal must start with getting married first—not a small project. Actually, come to think of it, competition existed among the women. I certainly took part in it. That competition gave us lots of status and ego. I used to feel so good about myself, and your father was proud, too." She always refers to my dad as "your father."

"Ma, I am dying here," I said. "Tell me about the women competing among themselves. What was that if it wasn't about the shape of your bodies and the size of your boobs? Was it about social status and not sex appeal gimmicks? Are you sure about feeling competitive?" I thought I wasn't making myself clear, but she understood.

She finally answered, from half way across the world, from decades of genuine feminine history in the making. "It wasn't the size of your breasts and not the size of your waist either. It was the size of your baby!"

How could I forget! Those childhood stories and my baby pictures. The bigger the baby, the bigger the proof of feminine authenticity. I was breast-fed for over twelve months and was considered to be a huge baby. (Gee, thanks mom.) My mother used to tell me how the nurses at the well-baby clinic would ask her to bring me over to their parenting classes for show-and-tell to demonstrate how good a healthy baby should look. In those days, the well-baby clinics were actually whale-baby clinics.

Size was, indeed, everything.

Chapter Four

SILICONE *Valley*

Four Weeks Later

Breasts are a source of female pride and sexual identification, but they are also a source of competition, confusion, insecurity, and shame.

—from *Femininity,* by Susan Brownmiller

Femaleness and its sexuality are beautiful. Women have long secretly suspected as much. In that sexuality, women are physically beautiful already; superb; breathtaking.

—from *The Beauty Myth,* by Naomi Wolf

ONE OF MY FAVORITE PLACES FOR OBSERVING HUMAN BEHAVIOR is in a large grocery store. I like being surrounded by fabulous edibles. My love of food feeds more than my body; it also feeds my psyche—and my soul. One day, on an analyst's couch when I was the patient, I connected those dots: my experiences of breast-feeding my sons to that love I felt through my mother's milk, and with my mother feeding and holding me. To me, my mother's breasts, her act of breast-feeding and holding, was heaven on earth. And so was feeding my own babies.

We are surrounded by primal symbols everywhere. I walk down the aisles of the grocery store, in love with the abundance and feeling what I can only describe as an appetite for life.

After a few minutes in the supermarket aisles, however, I often become desensitized to the colors, shapes, and commercial inducements. The American art of marketing becomes a blur, but people come more clearly into focus. Their behaviors are simple and interesting. Probably this is one of the most unrealistic places for thinking and speculating. Yet, over the years, this place—my neighborhood supermarket—has become a ground for new ideas as I observe people during their little routines each week. I look past the marketing traps and concentrate on small, mundane human interactions.

My favorite subjects are parents and their children. I like to watch the fascinating dynamics of mature adults who have to bargain their way out of the store, wresting control from their young in every aisle. We've all seen parents ultimately give in to a three-year-old who has mounted a campaign of terror against them in public.

So much goes on in a supermarket. In one aisle, near the meat section, I watched a young couple negotiate what to choose for dinner that night. The young woman was forceful and her husband acquiesced to purchase turkey for the evening meal. All of these characters play parts in a human drama. I imagine the mother who I had just seen, the one who was manipulated by her three-year-old daughter, giving in to the girl and empowering her daughter with certain values, just as the young man had given in to his wife. I stretched my fantasy to picture the young woman as a three-year-old negotiating with her mother in a supermarket aisle twenty years earlier.

I moved on to the produce section. As I considered my selections, Lisa, Rosie, Angela, Isabel, Tina, and many of my female patients from the past paraded through my mind. They could fill a small auditorium, I thought. What is it we all want?

Someone bumped into my cart and I heard myself apologizing. Mistake, I thought, and in my mind I took my apology back and decided not to feel badly about it.

This trip to the grocer's was great. I remembered to get almost everything I wanted. And I only got one thing that I absolutely didn't need—some sesame seed crackers.

The imaginary crowd of women in my head would not leave, so they all came home with me. I invited them to help me put the produce away and proceeded to my library where an old friend came to the rescue. I let myself get into the reading and had the imaginary crowd of women in my mind listen along.

In *Presentation of Gender* by Robert Stoller, M.D., I read:

> Masculinity or femininity is a belief—more precisely, a dense mass of beliefs. An American Indian warrior wore his hair long and felt masculine; a Prussian represented his claim to manliness with very short hair. Masculinity is not measured by hair length but by a person's conviction that long or short hair is masculine.

Stoller explains the development of core gender identity:

> In all mammals, including humans, anatomic maleness cannot occur without the addition of fetal androgens... This newer view of gender identity holds that femininity in females is not just penis envy or denial or resigned

acceptance of castration; a woman is not just a failed man. Masculinity in males is not simply a natural state that needs only to be defended if it is to grow healthily; rather, it is an achievement.

For the next two weeks the group struggled with definitions around issues of femininity. On occasion we were fortunate to be able to examine some more resources and share our readings. The first progress I noted about the group was that they had stopped using terms such as "becoming more feminine." Instead, they had advanced to "being feminine" and the therapeutic "feeling feminine" (or not feeling feminine). The difference might not seem that important, but it brought a noticeable relief for some of the women.

For Rosie and Lisa, for instance, the validation of their femininity was a major event in their psychological growth. They were able to feel relief in the way they perceived themselves. In a case like Rosie's, I usually noted less self-deprecation. In Lisa, there was less grandiosity and maybe even the beginning of empathy.

A great deal of valuable wisdom changed hands among us. Another one of the pearls came from Dr. Northrup's book *Women's Bodies, Women's Wisdom:*

> The cultural imperative that judges a woman's worth by her attachment to a man and by her sexual attractiveness to men—all men—runs very deep. Far too many women have internalized the culturally sanctioned sexual habits and needs of men as their own, when in fact male sexuality and sexual needs are probably more different and varied than we've all been led to believe.

After hearing this, Tina noticed the words "sexual attractiveness," and she immediately identified attractiveness with large breasts. Lisa, Rosie, Angela, Isabel, and Pat agreed with Tina.

Energetic conversations about sexual attractiveness had become an obvious concern to this group. On many occasions, the women had attempted to understand, or at least define, this phenomenon. We concluded that sexual attractiveness is a subjective experience, dependent to some extent on cultural and fashion influences. It also has significant meaning and value for each of us in our daily lives. When women discuss fashion and style, for example, they give a great deal of thought to what they consider to be "sexy" looking, whether they wish to emphasize or de-emphasize it. Energy, money, and imagination are all poured into our perception of sex appeal, they noted.

Regarding this, Rosie wanted to know how the rest of the group felt about the association of large breasts with attractiveness, so she went around the room asking each member. They agreed with her except for Beth, who felt that there was more to sexual attractiveness than large breasts.

"And what would that be?" Lisa asked.

"Well, for me, it's all in the *attitude*," Beth said. "You may have big breasts and a lousy attitude about your own sensuality, your own self-esteem. It's the attitude that is unattractive."

No one responded. The statement sounded profound to them. Then they looked at me, a situation I was very familiar with. They wanted a maternal validation. But as far as I was concerned, each woman needed to make up her own mind regarding values, so I was not about to say a word. Instead, I put on my "professional mask" and listened.

Katherine said, "Right, I'll go with that. I like it. Thanks, Beth."

"Yes, yes, we'll take it," someone else said.

"Now what do I do?" Isabel asked. "Do I need big breasts and a big attitude?"

"Yes, yes, yes" was the response from several of the women.

As they enjoyed a laugh, I decided to bring some therapy work back to the group.

"Tina, what first motivated you to say that sexual attractiveness means big breasts?"

Tina was a bit of an enigma in this group. She was an assertive, successful career woman. Her self-discipline in most areas of life was admirable. Her father emigrated from Japan where he had been very prosperous. Tina had often talked about him. There was always a question in our minds about this relationship, which seemed to embrace both intense love and intense hate.

Tina sat up straight in her chair, looking elegant as usual, and said, "The culture that I was raised in admires Western looks. The need to be exactly like Americans was all around me. In this group, I feel very much accepted as who I am. In the world out there, I've created—invented, if you will—my own rules, my own style, my own life."

Jane asked, "What do you mean 'you invented your own life'?"

Tina thought for a moment, and then said, "I think what I mean is that I was too little to understand what my father wanted. He planted us—my brothers, my mom, and me—in Los Angeles but often left us for business trips to Japan and Europe. I was seven years old and didn't speak any English when we moved here. He left for weeks at a time. Before his departure, my mother would be paralyzed with fear or hysterical with anger.

"He left me with wads of cash. Hundreds, maybe thousands of dollars each time. What I'm telling you is not a story of a poor refugee girl whose family had to sell their bodies for food. This is a story of a poor girl whose wealthy family had no roots any-where—no orientation to life, no identity to speak of. And maybe we sold our souls to have the American dream. The need to belong somewhere was immense.

"I'd started to figure out things for myself. I couldn't trust my mother who simply parroted my father. I think my mother was in culture shock. Thirty years later, she still is. She hardly spoke any English for years.

"I was the complete opposite. I found out about the power of money." Her face became animated, glowing with intensity, which it often did when she spoke about work, especially her work. "First, I learned to get more money out of my father. Later, I didn't want to ever need money from him. Since I was always a good student, I continued to study until I got my MBA. That part of life I knew how to do really well. I started my company while still in school. Like my father, I learned to give my job all of my attention."

Tina stopped talking and looked at the floor. For the first time she looked vulnerable.

"Tina, do you need me to remind you about the subject you started with?" I asked softly.

"I'm afraid I am becoming slow like my mother," she said without any sarcasm. "I know, I know…big boobs and attractiveness." She smiled for the first time in a long time. "The notion of being a business school graduate and a businesswoman has done wonders for my relationship with my father. What a concept. His own daughter is making it big in America." She paused. "I thrive on it too. Maybe pleasing him started it all. But who knows, perhaps I internalized his desires so well that I cannot distinguish them from my own.

"There is one area, though, that I cannot yet conquer. That is, of course, the area of femininity and sexuality. I cannot bring myself to feel like Beth. I'm slender and tall and I look all right in all my business suits, but I still don't feel sexy. Never did.

"I want to say that it is my lousy attitude, but if I'm honest with myself, I believe it is my flat chest or my Japanese build that is the problem. I wish I'd had my breasts enhanced surgically. I'm actually considering it. I think about it every morning in the shower." She stopped almost in the middle of a sentence.

Beth asked, "Why? Why do you think about it?"

"Because it's my private American dream," Tina said.

I felt a lump in my throat. For a moment I couldn't respond. This was so completely piercing. I swallowed as if that would get rid of my sadness. Beth wiped away some tears. Grace leaned over and gave Tina a long hug. Rosie was actually crying and Angela, who already had a red nose, held Pat and Isabel's hands.

At the next session in our New Information segment we shared a marvelous piece of learning from *Sexual Unfolding* by Lorna and Phillip Sarrel. At the beginning of the book is this note:

> The Sarrels point out that in the permissive and sexually charged atmosphere of college campuses and other social milieus of teenagers, some young people may bypass critical stages in their sexual-psychological-social growth.

There is an engaging description regarding our culture and breasts in the first chapter of this wonderful book.

> Girls worry about when they develop, their size and shape, the existence or nonexistence of hair around the areola, inverted nipples and breast asymmetry. Even in this era of liberated, braless young women and a concept of fashion that make small breasts an asset, masses of girls and women feel devastated by 'flat-chestedness.' We were made aware of the extent of concern about small breasts through a monthly magazine column we wrote. We kept a tally of questions asked and, much to our surprise, found that, second only to questions about female sex response and orgasm, were letters expressing a desire to have large breasts. In 1974–75, the total number of questions about the body was 161. Of these, 106 were about breasts. The letters vary from expression of mild concern to severe, almost crippling worry about lack of 'femininity' and sexual attractiveness because of small breasts. Feelings about breasts tended to generalize to feeling about the entire self, expressed in statements like, 'I have become obsessed that I am horrible.'

The following excerpt is typical of the feelings associated with this issue:

I have always had small breasts. It didn't concern me too much except I never dated any boy, always fearing they would notice if I went swimming. But now here's my biggest problem. Recently, I fell in love with a young man and he loves me and he brought up the subject of having sex. Sex! How can I let him see my ugly body, especially my breasts! God only knows if my breasts weren't so small and ugly I'd not think twice for I love him so, but I'm afraid of him seeing me. Will I ever get over this fear? I haven't consulted any doctor because I'm even afraid to let them see me! I feel so unfeminine and deprived especially when I see other girls who have nice breasts. I'm afraid I shall never be able to have a normal sex life.

The extent to which our culture has fetishized the breast as a symbol of female sexuality is well known and the woman who doesn't resemble a centerfold can suffer from lowered self-esteem because she doesn't, literally and figuratively, measure up. Research on body image has shown that there are shared group norms regarding ideal dimensions for body parts and that a person's attitude toward a body part is significantly determined by deviation of that part from the norm. But the young woman's feelings about small breasts cut much deeper than a need to compete in the arena of sexual attractiveness. The full breast has come to stand for all aspects of female sexuality, in particular, sexual responsiveness, although such a correlation has no basis in truth.

The group had not been together for an entire week. Tina, however, had stayed on my mind. My thoughts had nothing to do with her desire for fuller breasts but rather the discrepancy I had witnessed between her adult, high-functioning life and her emotional, psychological development. There was more human suffering to her life than having a flat chest.

Tina was forty or forty-one, although some of the women thought she was in her mid-twenties. She looked ageless. In intimate relationships, she acted like a beginner. It seemed a little odd to look at this youthful female, to hear her naiveté about personal and intimate relationships, and at the same time to know that she is a tough, successful businesswoman, far more successful than her father.

Tina was divorced, but was now dating again. She described her short marriage as lonely. She had married one of the executives in her company, but she did not know how to separate business from intimacy. The marriage was merely an extension of her office life. There was, in fact, no intimacy, no passion. She said that she had no idea how to be a wife, and her mother's example was unacceptable to her. She went all the way to the other extreme and modeled herself after her father. Or so she thought. But that only worked effectively in business. When she got married and later divorced, she treated it as a merger or an acquisition. Divorce was not a trauma for her, but rather "a loss I had to take," as she put it.

Even after being divorced for two years, Tina still did not view her recent history as a segment of human relations with its own dynamics from which she could garner some wisdom. Her conclusion was that she was not "feminine" enough.

Consequently, she considered her contribution to the marriage relationship "defective." She was too flat-chested, unattractive, and unworthy. The damage to her individuality was great, and Tina was unable to see herself as a whole woman.

During the next session, Tina showed a great deal of appreciation for the members of the group. She was touched by our interest in her history. She was also ready to contribute to our education. That day, we learned some of her history we had not known before.

"I left the group last week with so many emotions and thoughts," Tina continued. "Over the weekend it hit me. No one had asked me why I hadn't already had my boobs done."

"Are you serious?" said Beth. "I wouldn't want to suggest that solution."

"I know. I was just sharing that I noticed that. However, I'm still obsessed with the idea. Let me tell you some history. I've been reading about implants for a few years now, and you know I'm a researcher. Listen." She was somber. She pulled out a book with many Post-It notes attached to it. The book was *Science on Trial*, by Marcia Angell, M.D. executive editor of the prestigious *New England Journal of Medicine*. Tina read:

> The first known attempt to enlarge a woman's breasts occurred in Germany in 1895. (Interestingly, surgery to reduce breast size had been performed for many years.) In that first operation, fat from a benign tumor on the woman's back was transplanted to her breasts. Within a few years, surgeons were experimenting with paraffin wax to enlarge breasts. Later, other foreign substances were tried, including petroleum jelly, beeswax, and vegetable oils, but paraffin remained the mainstay. Probably the first women to turn to silicone were Japanese prostitutes after World War II, trying to satisfy the taste of American occupation forces for Western-style large breasts. Instead of having discrete packets of silicone surgically implanted in their breasts, as is now done, these women had liquid silicone or paraffin injected by needle or tube directly into their breast tissue, often along with assorted contaminants. Within a few years, breast augmentation by silicone injection had spread to the United States, where it found particular favor among Las Vegas showgirls and aspiring actresses in California.
>
> In general, silicone elicits only a very mild inflammatory response. But when large amounts of liquid silicone were

injected directly into the breast, as was done to the Japanese prostitutes, there were often terrible consequences. Bacterial contamination from dirty needles or contaminated silicone was common. It wasn't just silicone that was being injected, but all manner of other substances and bacteria. A severe inflammatory reaction often formed around each tiny globule of silicone, making the breasts lumpy and hard, particularly as the scar tissue contracted. Because the liquid silicone tended to migrate into the soft tissue around the breasts or in the armpit, it was customary to add irritating substances, such as olive oil, so that there would be even more scar tissue to trap the silicone and anchor it in place. The scarring around silicone globules could then become so severe that it produced grotesque lumps that resembled tumors. In addition, when the breasts become infected, gangrenous sores sometimes developed on the overlying skin or nipple. Needless to say, besides being disfiguring, the complications of directly injecting silicone were often excruciatingly painful.

Some education.

None of us had known about the kind of suffering those women had gone through. Nonetheless, the point was not only about these women and their tale. In our unfolding story, this was about Tina's evolution. Her reading choices made so much sense that she became almost transparent to us.

Isabel picked up on it quickly. Her immediate reaction was to say it was gory, but then she reached further and asked, "Why did you choose to do this particular reading? Is it because of the prostitution part?"

Tina looked around the room in disbelief. She would not answer for a while, then said, "Prostitution? What are you saying to me?"

Isabel was startled a bit by this reaction "I didn't wish to offend you. I appreciate your courageous act of finding this material and giving us this gift. I'm more concerned with you than the story. I'm concerned with the connection you made between the Japanese female physical build, sexuality, and yourself."

"Tina," I said, "focus back on the elements that Isabel suggested. She is caring about you. Even if it is uncomfortable, you can handle the pain. You are fine."

Tina went along. "I hear what you're saying—that I am binding together my physical disposition with the prostitutes' solution for their flat-chested reality."

"Yes, you got it." Isabel sighed.

"Wait," I said quickly while she was not defensive. "There is more. May I?"

Tina smiled. "Like I've a choice here?"

"Thanks," I said casually, participating in the inside joke, appreciating the trust.

"Yes, you are binding together, as you said, the prostitutes' thesis about what is sexually attractive on the market with how you feel about yourself. It's not really about your physical disposition, though. It concerns how you feel about it. How you *feel* about your body."

"Tell me more, and in English this time," Tina shot back.

"With pleasure. You mentioned the part regarding the prostitutes' silicone injections as a solution. Well, there is a delicate matter here. The prostitutes are working girls. However, with all respect to professionalism, their decision to enlarge their breasts does not make you, Tina, who is also Japanese, a sexually unattractive woman. You've combined your ambition for sexual attractiveness with the standards of a prostitute who is not enriching her sexual pleasure. She is a working girl. It's her job. Not her pleasure!" I stressed. "In your associations, in the back of your mind, there is a mix-up of definitions. You've mixed up sexuality with work and selling a product, which you confuse with a negative outlook about breast size, which has merged together with being Japanese a long time ago. English enough?"

"English enough." She gave me one of her rare smirks, then looked at Isabel and thanked her. "I need to think about it some more."

"Of course," I said. "Take your time."

There was a lot of discussion that day. Most of the women wanted to talk about the readings and to imagine what life had been like for the Japanese prostitutes. Jane and Rosie wanted more clarifications regarding the explanation I gave Tina. Grace wanted to know more about how things can get mixed up in one's mind and create some erroneous values. Angela was interested in finding out more about the issues of sexuality, pleasure, and the ability to tell them apart. Generally, the message regarding femininity was getting clearer.

The very next session started with questions and answers about the story of the Japanese women. I had also been thinking about it.

Not surprisingly, Grace came ready with yet another book, *Informed Consent* by John A. Byrne. Grace suggested that her selected reading, however, might be redundant. No, no, the women protested; they all wanted to hear what she had brought.

> In the aftermath of World War II, transformer coolant made of silicone was suddenly disappearing from the docks of Yokohama Harbor in Japan. The silicone fluid was used by cosmeticians to enlarge the small breasts of Asian prostitutes who knew that a more Western appearance would enhance their appeal to American serviceman. Larger doses of the doctored industrial fluids were injected directly into their breasts.

> Long before electronic gadgets and Toyotas, silicone injections became one of the first successful Japanese

exports into America. The practice traveled immediately to Nevada, California and Texas, where mostly exotic dancers sought out the procedure to increase the size of their breasts. Some doctors charged as much as $1,000 to inject the fluid between the pectoral muscles of the chest wall and the back of the mammary tissues—a technique that became known as the 'Sakurai formula' after a doctor who originated the practice in Japan. Dr. Sakurai moved to Beverly Hills, where he opened up a clinic and helped popularize the injections in the United States. By 1965, the Food and Drug Administration estimated that at least 75 doctors offered the treatment in Los Angeles alone. A doctor in Las Vegas crowed to Newsweek that he had given some 16,000 silicone injections to 200 women. Silicone 'pampers' trekked into Las Vegas to set up walk-in clinics in hotels along the strip. Complications due to injections soared so rapidly that in 1975 Nevada enacted emergency legislation making silicone injections a felony punishable by one to six years' imprisonment and a $10,000 fine. A year later, California passed a similar law making silicone breast injections a misdemeanor.

We left that session wondering why women would volunteer to risk their lives or health and flaunt the law. The group was touched by the story and suggested new questions to address in future sessions. Some of their questions were:

- Was our culture demanding sexual attractiveness at all costs?
- Has our culture defined sexual attractiveness as large breasts?
- Are large breasts the ticket that must be bought by females who wish to be attractive?
- Since large breasts were not the standard of beauty sixty or seventy years ago, what had happened to our perception?
- Who had done it to us? Or had we done it to ourselves?

Chapter Five

BOSOM *Buddies*

Four Weeks Later

Because she is forced to concentrate on the minutiae of her bodily parts, a woman is never free of self-consciousness.

—from *Femininity*, by Susan Brownmiller

I find it interesting that the ovaries, the uterus, and the breasts are practically the only organs taken out to prevent cancer. This attitude finds its way into both the privacy of the doctor's office and the medical literature: one prominent Boston surgeon wrote in the Journal of Clinical Surgery *that he believed in 'tossing the excess baggage overboard to keep the ship of life afloat.' He was speaking only of breasts; it would be interesting to learn whether he considered testicles to be excess baggage.*

—from *The Woman Source Catalog and Review,* edited by Ilene Rosoff

I WOULD SOON BE THREE YEARS SINCE PAT'S MOTHER HAD died. Pat had a tremendous feeling of loss in her life and she was not finished grieving, in spite of the anguish she'd been experiencing for many months. Pat was thirty years old. Since her mother's death, she had become familiar with psychotherapy as a process. She joined this group by referral from her therapist—a grief therapist who felt that Pat would benefit from another kind of therapeutic process. The therapist told Pat that since "normal grieving time" had long since passed, she needed new exposure. Pat came in willingly. She was lost in anger, sadness, and a preoccupation with the absence of her mother, Susan.

Pat used to describe Susan to us on every occasion, so we found out a great deal about her. We knew Susan to be a progressive woman who was active in charities, women's causes, and political issues. Susan was assertive, physically fit, open-minded, and from what Pat said, charismatic. Susan was an accomplished reporter and writer. When she died, she was fifty-four years old.

We heard about her nearly every week, at times in cries and other times in whispers. We felt the presence of this woman through her daughter's pain. In the last few years of Susan's life, mother and daughter had become good friends, which intrigued certain members of the group. Rosie, Lisa, and Tina were introduced to a new level of intimacy with one's mom. Grace enjoyed these moments when Pat spoke about her mother, since the conversations brought up thoughts of her own relationship with her daughter Amy.

The beauty of group work is that when a single member shares, so many levels of the psychotherapy process occur simultaneously. When a person talks about her pain, one might identify with her, another might recognize her spouse or a family member or friend, and still another will gain new insight into an old issue. Results can speed up considerably when more people are sharing a problem.

Pat was the one to introduce us to the book *The Body Project,* by Joan Jacobs Brumberg, in which the author describes relationships between mothers and daughters. I found it especially interesting since the book covers historical and anthropological issues of development in young girls. Brumberg writes:

> In the twentieth century the body has become the central personal project of American girls. This priority makes girls today vastly different from their Victorian counterparts. Although girls in the past and present display many common developmental characteristics—such as self-consciousness, sensitivity to peers, and an interest in establishing an independent identity—before the twentieth century, girls simply did not organize their thinking about themselves around their bodies. Today, many young girls worry about the contours of their bodies—especially shape, size, and muscle tone—because they believe that the body is the ultimate expression of the self.
>
> The body is a consuming project for contemporary girls because it provides an important means of self-definition, a way to visibly announce who you are to the world. From a historical perspective, this particular form of adolescent expression is a relatively recent phenomenon. In the twentieth century, adolescent girls learned from their mothers, as well as from the larger culture, that modern femininity required some degree of exhibitionism.
>
> By the 1920s, both fashion and film had encouraged a massive 'unveiling' of the female body, which meant that certain body parts—such as arms and legs—were bared and displayed in ways they had never been before. This new freedom to display the body was accompanied, however, by demanding beauty and dietary regimens that involved money as well as self-discipline. Beginning in the 1920s, women's legs and underarms had to be smooth and free of body hair; the torso had to be svelte;

the breasts were supposed to be small and firm. What American women did not realize at the time was that their stunning new freedom actually implied the need for greater internal control of the body, an imperative that would intensify and become even more powerful by the end of the twentieth century.

The seeds of this cultural and psychological change from external to internal control of the body lie in vast societal transformations that characterized the move from agrarian to industrial society and from a religious to a secular world.

The book *The Body Project* appealed to all of us for a variety of reasons. Some of us liked the historical perspectives on girls' development. Others needed to establish for themselves some norms and standards since they had been raised with chaotic modeling of what femininity is or is not. It was obvious that Isabel, Lisa, Rosie, Angela, and Pat had formal education in what was called "health" in schools and is now "sex education." Others in our group were too old to have had this education, so *The Body Project* was a good educational supplement for them.

One paragraph in the book captured Angela's attention. It dealt with separate body parts, how each part was examined, measured, and compared. Angela focused on it.

Breasts are particularly important to girls in cultures or time periods that give powerful meaning or visual significance to that part of the body. Throughout history, different body parts have been eroticized in art, literature, photography, and film. In some eras, the ankle or upper arm was the ultimate statement of female sexuality. But breasts were the particular preoccupation of Americans in the years after World War II, when voluptuous stars, such as Jayne Mansfield, Katherine Russell, and Marilyn Monroe, were popular box-office attractions. The mammary fixation of the 1950s extended beyond movie stars and shaped the experience of adolescents of both genders. In that era boys seemed to prefer girls who were 'busty,' and American girls began to worry about breast size as well as about weight.

Angela confessed that body parts were her preoccupation since childhood. She was interested to know if anyone else had those feelings. Before anyone could answer, I intervened and asked Angela about the importance of those body parts to her. Also when were they important and *why?*

She squirmed in her seat. Finally, she said, "I've never seen any psychological meaning in my interest in body parts. I guess I'm responding to what was positively reinforced in my childhood. Actually, I'm not sure about that. I think about my childhood on many occasions while others here are working on their issues. Especially during the sessions when Lisa, Isabel, Tina, and Rosie are sharing, I get reeducated about my childhood. It's easier for me to hear others' stories and then look inside myself to see where I stand. I learned long ago that every time I got attention for my little performances at home, in front of my father, I perceived that behavior as significant and went for more of the same.

"My dad had no active interest in the kids. He was tired and preoccupied and wanted to be left alone to watch the news or sports. But I could get some energy rise from him when I did some unusual act. He was easily bored with basic kids' talk, like my sisters'. They brought home the regular stuff, games, gossip, and assignments from school.

"I'd grown to understand the power of my performance acts. Each time I'd display a new move, a new jump, a new dance, I was applauded. I excelled in dressing up and moving or standing and displaying. For a while, the activity was about the things I was showing, the scarves, the necklaces, hats, and sandals. Later as I became aware of myself, it was about a collection of parts that worked together as a system.

"Each part was tested and retested. No wonder I make a good living modeling today. It paid me many times over." She paused. "Except in one area. I'll never forget that my own dad, who was supposed to be so proud of me, didn't show up for my graduation. He did, however, for years travel to my modeling shows."

"So, Angela," Beth said, "you'd learned over the years to show and focus on body parts. You had to enjoy the process. Let me ask you something." Beth looked into Angela's eyes. "Are you familiar with the expression 'the whole is greater than the sum of its parts'?"

"Yes," said Angela. The rest of us smiled at Beth's attempt to educate that was so transparent.

"I was just wondering," continued Beth, not seeing the humor in the situation, "if you see how this applies to your own life."

"I'll think about it," Angela said and smiled. "Maybe you've got something there." The rest of us smiled with her.

My favorite part in *The Body Project* is the description of the history of the bra. It mentions a one-piece camisole of the 1900s, which I remember from period films. It didn't do much for breast enhancement, but looked very feminine. Historically, bras were designed with the purpose to show a **flat** upper body. Later on, as late as the 1930s, the idea of showing and enhancing the roundness of the breast started to emerge.

When it was first pointed out to the group that eighty or ninety years ago women were actually hand-making their own underwear, it generated a lively discussion. The women were fascinated. How would it look today to make homemade bras? Would we dare wear them? What kinds of materials, colors, styles, textures, and accessories would we use?

As I look back on these sessions, I realized that the reaction to this handmade-bras information was extraordinary. As far as I know, there was no contact among the group members during the week. Yet, for reasons that I'll explore later, some energy moved each one of them in the same direction. In an informal way, not deliberately, the women added spirituality to an ordinary daily activity—women exploring the history of underwear! Being a part of such a process was an amazing experience.

Psychologist Carl Jung coined the term for this phenomenon: the "collective unconscious." He believed there is an energy and mental process that is unconscious, transcends barriers of cultures and genders. And our group experienced that collective intense reaction to a brief discussion about the history of bras.

Tina made a suggestion that we make a few handmade items, too, just to see what it would feel like. The idea sparked a great deal of interest. I had to spoil the fun and say that this was not the standard group therapy procedure. They seemed to understand my concern. A minute later, Grace said, "How about if we bring in some plain bras and decorate them with embroidery? How about that?"

"Grace, this is group...." I tried to protest.

"I know, I know," Lisa jumped in. "We'll bring the stuff in and we'll stay after group. How is that?"

Each of the group members took turns announcing her enthusiastic agreement to staying after group for arts and crafts. The pressure was on me. From being a professional group leader, I became a party pooper. However, we agreed to a one-hour stay-over for a limited number of weeks. I suggested four weeks and was overruled. Eight weeks was the final agreement.

What actually took place was rather simple. Each week after the session for one hour, the women become involved in an old-fashioned, craft project. They sat on chairs or on the carpet, cutting, sewing, and measuring but mainly having lively supportive conversation.

Their first project idea was suggested by Grace. They brought in some samples of new bras they bought for the occasion. During the hour, they added embroidery, pearls, and lace, creating finished products that were surprisingly beautiful.

This was a wonderful opportunity for me to see these women as friends. They were playful, ingenious, fun loving, and completely focused on the process of creation.

Over the eight weeks, each woman expressed herself in her own unique way. The store-bought bras didn't satisfy their sense of authenticity. Collectively, they decided the garments had to be handmade!

For Jane, this was a great opportunity to demonstrate her sewing ability to deftly restore old garments. Hers was not just a skill but also a definite talent. Not many can take an old garment and recycle it into a contemporary, imaginative design. By doing this she had rediscovered a part of herself. Grace was in heaven. Her entire demeanor changed. She loved the informal interactions with the "ladies," as she called us.

Isabel had a magical touch when it came to selecting luxurious and rare fabrics of sheer and lacy quality, many of them reflecting distant cultures.

Katherine suggested documenting their creative work and volunteered to take pictures and make a videotape.

The creative occupation of hand making feminine undergarments was filled with humor too.

Jane lifted a garment and said jokingly, "I wonder what Freud would've had to say about this?"

"What do you have there, Jane?" Tina asked.

"Well, for now it's nothing, but it's going to be a pretty pink slip," Jane said, excited about the prospect.

"Don't worry about Freud," I said. "We'll simply call it a Freudian slip." And with that everyone in the room cracked up.

I should add that this project was done with no leader or director. The spirit was democratic; everything was carried out with mutual respect, consideration, and kindness. This process bore no resemblance to any group therapy I'd ever seen. The joy, creativity, and self-expression made it as healing as play therapy, plus one of the most energizing moments for this group since its inception.

This playfulness was highly therapeutic; however, other aspects of innocence and spontaneity emerged. These included:

- an expression of creativity
- a "smooth" regression to childlike playfulness
- a getting-in-touch-with femininity
- a recreation of sensuality
- a rebuilding of feminine self-image
- a developing of a strong spiritual connection
- and last but hardly least, the creation of a sisterhood and cohesive group feeling.

Sharing specific life experiences while hand making underwear was therapeutic and healing. As in quilting when women sit together at a task, they openly exchanged intimate stories. The most interesting stories were about first bra experiences. I found them indicative to the relationship each woman had with her own breasts past and present.

The experience of reclaiming one's femininity, reshaping attitudes, and actually designing bras and undergarments made an intense impression on these women. They kept sharing with each other long-past pleasures and lessons they had learned from mothers, grandmothers, and extended family members. The effort to revive an all-women turn-of-the-century practice became a celebration.

Many weeks later we heard from two of our group members, Rosie and Beth, who continued our ideas. They had instituted afternoon activities with their neighbors and their daughters and nieces, telling stories and making women's undergarments. Last we heard, one of these groups named themselves Wonder Bras Girls; another group became The Bosom Buddies.

As for the rest of the history lesson, it was a slow progress as *The Body Project* documented. It is stated in the book that the transition from homemade to mass-produced bras was critical in how adolescent girls thought about their breasts. For as soon as girls could buy those ready-made bras, the style and fashion were taken away from their mothers.

The same chapter describes how store-bought clothes do not always fit the human body and how women had to use the mass-produced bras. When young women did not fit into the standard sizes they felt that there was something wrong with their bodies. Interestingly, the mass-produced bras did give a sense of autonomy from family tradition, and at the same time, increased self-consciousness about breasts.

There are other perspectives on the use of bras. Here is one from *Dr. Susan Love's Breast Book:*

> In our society breasts and their coverings have become almost a fetish. The bra is a relatively recent invention—it became popular in the 1920s. As a replacement for the uncomfortable and often mutilating corsets of the 19th century, it was certainly an improvement. However, although wearing a bra is never physically harmful, it has no medical necessity whatsoever.

Later on in her book, Dr. Love gets into areas we had yet not touched on. Namely, myths and realities about the role of bras in the health and look of breasts. She maintains that breasts will sag because of the proportion of fat contents, not because of bra size.

> No one type of bra is better or worse for you in terms of health. Some of my patients wear underwire bras and are told they can get cancer from them. This is nonsense. It makes no difference medically whether your bra opens in the front or back, is padded or not padded.

As the sewing and measuring went on, the conversation picked up on appearances and grooming habits.

Jane said, "I'm really having a bad hair day! Sorry, girls, you know what I mean."

Tina jumped in and said that she felt the same last week. There was an atmosphere of acceptance. As if each one had been there before.

I requested a clarification. "What exactly do you mean by having a bad hair day?" As if I did not know. Some of the women jumped in with the obvious comments about managing their hair.

"What about it?" I asked. The responses were unanimous. It is hard to trust your hair, for it has its own personality. Each day, it might behave independently of our wishes and needs. I made a comment that the idea is bizarre, considering that hair is a human organism growing from our bodies.

Then I asked, "What do you suggest we do about it?"

Several ideas were brought up, from conditioning, shampooing, coloring, to cutting or styling it. We also agreed that there was an ongoing relationship with our own hair. From this moment on, the relevance became clear. The manner in which we spoke about the management of our hair was indicative of the quality of the relationship we have with it.

Rosie objected saying, "But relationships are a mutual thing."

Angela replied, "Absolutely. My hair responds to my manipulations and I react to its behavior."

"Does anyone see the relevance to breasts?" Beth, the born teacher who was reading my mind, asked that question.

But Lisa impulsively jumped in and took over. "I'm sure having a good boob day every day." The comic relief came too soon.

I called us back to order and pulled that train of thought out of the unscheduled station. "Relationships," I began. "The point is the relationship that we do not have with our breasts! We've just heard about the intricate mutual dependency we have with our hair. So it is with our teeth, our skin, our nails, and our weight. But what about our breasts? Can you see how the majority of us have negative relationships with our breasts? Remember Lisa before the implants? Remember Rosie's reaction? Amy's? Tina's? Pat's?"

The silence in the room was deafening as they processed the message. Beth had a little smile on her face. She got it. Katherine looked directly at me. Her eyes met mine and she relaxed. She got it too. Isabel looked down at her breasts, then up at me, and giggled. She was in.

As for the rest of the group, Tina looked down at the floor. Grace crossed her hands under her chest and looked down. Lisa was fidgeting in her chair. Pat seemed puzzled. Jane was busy looking at Angela. And there was Angela. She looked sad, and I thought for a moment she was crying. I made a mental note of each one's reaction.

Katherine started slowly, "I guess you've got something there. Let me see. Do I hear you say that, overall, we don't have a relationship with our breasts?"

"Or that we don't have a good enough relationship with them?" Isabel added.

"Or that we could have a loving relationship with those two?" Beth was laughing with pleasure.

I agreed and congratulated them on their responses. I felt the groundwork was laid for this particular learning process.

"My life goal for now is to teach you this simple attitude: We need to establish positive relationships with our precious breasts. I mean it in the physical as well as emotional and spiritual senses. Breasts are susceptible to our attitudes. So let's start our positive outlook today. I personally have nothing against breast implants or other improvements."

"Too bad," said Beth who was trying to promote her war against implants.

I motioned her to wait. "I have a problem, though, with put downs, name calling, self-deprecations, and lack of self-love. I don't want you to get an idea that I'm lecturing here for or against push-up bras or implants. The point is your attitude." I knew I had their full attention.

"I would like to propose an attitude upgrade today," I stated seriously.

But they laughed and Grace volunteered this explanation: "You have this spark in your eyes when you talk and we know that something unusual is coming. Isn't it so?" She looked at me and smiled.

"Right." I finally gave in to her persistence. "Here is what I propose. From this day on, instead of belittling and putting down our breasts, we each honor them and give them affectionate names. Give then endearing nicknames." The women roared with laughter.

Were they laughing at my idea? Well not exactly. As I was explaining the concept, Lisa was already into the "act." She was pointing at her breasts with her two thumbs and whispered, "Twin Peaks." It was funny indeed.

Beth volunteered to go next and suggested naming her breasts "Lucy" and "Ethel," her favorite leading ladies. The group applauded.

They liked the pattern of naming their breasts after famous shows and movie titles and moved into the game with ease.

Tina, sitting at the edge of her seat, raised her voice, "I know, I know! 'American Beauty' for my American dream." She was not kidding, but we laughed at her wit.

Katherine, who is usually calm and collected, seemed playful and jumped right in. "My breasts go with me to the hospital daily. They see the others' neglect and abuse. I'm scared for women. I'll call mine 'Working Girls' until prevention is practiced by all." Katherine put her right hand on her chest while she was talking.

"I hear you," Jane responded to Katherine. "I had a funny name for my breasts but I want to do this with sincerity. I realize more and more that my mental health depends on my attitude. I'll name my breasts 'Beloved' from now on."

The hand that rose in the air was Rosie's. She didn't look up. "I still don't like my body. I'm at war with it; 'The War of the Roses' is my name for my breasts for now."

This was getting serious. The names indicated the mental state of the group members. Now there was tension in the room.

Grace felt a need to mention her daughter, Amy, "I have two sets of breasts' names; one for me: 'Milk' and 'Honey' and another set for Amy: 'Tea for Two,' since her breasts will not be giving milk any time soon." She was sad.

Beth nudged Pat. She looked at her and reluctantly said, "OK, already. I'll name them 'Little Women,' my favorite childhood book."

The comic relief came from Isabel. "I remember how I discovered women's boobs on the beach, on the French Riviera, I felt very adventurous, I'll name them 'Thelma' and 'Louise,' from the movie. I really like this game."

Tina announced, "We didn't hear from Angela yet. Hey, Ange, name your tune!"

Angela smiled and replied, "Well, my breasts will be named 'The Replacements.' There, I said it."

Tina jumped right back. "What a strange name for your boobs."

Angela rolled her eyes and said, "I know. It's an old family joke, I'll tell you another time. Trust me."

I was about to start the next activity for the group when Rosie got up and said to me, "Wait a minute, what about your name? After all, it was your idea."

"Right on," Tina chimed in. "What do you call your breasts, Dr. Nili?"

"Well, why not." I dismissed the notion of privacy as their therapist. "Mine are named after 'Lady' and the 'Tramp' and they take turns changing roles." I joined in the laughs and motion for them to settle down to work with me. I proceeded to prepare the group to a guided imagery journey. A few cleansing breaths later and the room was relaxed again. Guided imagery exercises have become popular because they bring a dimension of spirituality and healing to the group process.

"I would like you to sit comfortably—you know, uncross your legs, shake out your limbs, relax. Take some deep breaths." I was finally moving them into the guided imagery session. The group went along with me. They got comfortable and took their time relaxing.

"Now, everyone look at your chest. On your chest, outside your rib cage, dwell these organs called breasts. Take a good look at them. Now close your eyes. Continue to breathe slowly and look at your chest with the inner eyes of your mind. Let your mind's eyes see your real breasts. Relax. Breathe slowly and luxuriously. Take in lots of air and take your time.

"Here, near your heart, are the organs we are meditating about. These are the same organs you first felt on your mother's chest as she held you, marveling over you minutes after you were born. They are also one of the first places most of us were nourished as our mothers cradled us.

"Relax. Breathe in generously and stretch your hands out. Now, very slowly, put your hands on your heart. Feel the life pumping there and enjoy the energy. This is the heart that you respect each day. You nurture its health, you are careful with its maintenance, and you attribute to it enormous responsibilities in your emotional life. Outside your very important heart dwell a woman's breasts.

"Continue to breathe slowly and relax. Enjoy the rhythmic pulse of your heart. Imagine those breasts again. They were not always with you, you know. For the first ten, eleven, twelve, or even thirteen years of your life, you did not have your breasts. One day they were budding. The next day they were blooming and blossoming. To some of us, they were growing faster than we did. To others, they stopped growing while our feet still increased in shoe size.

"Listen to your heart beat and notice your breasts. Those breasts are alive. Treat them well and they will help you stay healthy. Learn to accept them and love them. Remember these bosoms next to your heart. Practice and make them your friends.

You're your bosom's buddies; you know you cannot leave home without them. Take them everywhere with you with pride. And especially bring them home to your heart, in your consciousness. Carry them home lovingly as an integrated part of yourself.

"Your breasts are not a symbolic artifact that stands in for femininity. Your breasts are living organs of your female body. Those human tissues that make a breast are very vulnerable parts of the female anatomy. Respect them. Check and test them frequently. Talk to them like you would to plants or pets or other lovely living things. Enjoy the softness of the skin that envelops your breasts and notice the texture of your nipples. Embrace them as you would your own child. In fact, give them a loving nickname.

"And now it is time for a long hug from your loving arms to your beloved breasts. As you hug this pair of friends, thank them for being there, healthy and available for your needs.

"When you are finished saying thank you, please open your eyes."

They did. Ten women were hugging their chests, whispering softly to the breasts they had just gotten reacquainted with. Ten faces were flushed with great energy. Ten pairs of eyes were looking nowhere in particular, and ten pairs of hands lightly dried streams of tears. Actually, there were eleven, as I felt my own wet face.

The very next morning I had a chance to practice what I preach. Stretching on my stomach on the Pilates Reformer during a workout session, I noticed how the hard surface was pressing against my chest. In the past I would have moaned and groaned and complained about the size of my breasts. I would blame them for intruding on my fitness endeavor. This morning was different; I heard myself softly apologizing to my breasts for distressing them into this tough position. The good feeling from last night's session was lingering on, permeating my attitude towards my breast. I was on my way to a booby-trapped free life!

Chapter Six

Double BREASTED

Five Weeks Later

In our role as archaeologists of ourselves, every clue counts, and in the spiritual world, nothing is for drill and no experience is wasted.

> —from *Something More,*
>   by Sarah Ban Breathnach

When asked what place corsets can have in the 1990s, after three decades of women's liberation, fashion designer Donna Karan reported: 'You always get to the point where one part of the body is played up—and now it's the bust.'

> —from *A History of the Breast,*
>   by Marilyn Yalom

S THE WEEKS PASSED, THE WOMEN IN THE GROUP GOT ON WITH their lives, which were as varied as the group's participants. There were promotions, graduations, a grand opening of a branch store, a bankruptcy, and the launching of a new business. One married off a child, another started dating a new man, still another had a minor car accident, another found a new home, and some made new best friends or lost or gained lots of weight. They also experienced a European vacation, the falling out of love, and the placement of a parent in a home for the aged.

Without exception, though, in each session some reference was made to women's breasts. One week, it centered on breast cancer as an epidemic. The next week, several women talked about some new shapes of bras they were experimenting with. Another time, it was Lisa reporting about her adjustment to her new breasts.

This group paid more attention to breasts than any other group I had been with. I often thought this had to do with my own interest. Was I so booby-trapped that I could consistently listen to these thoughts, complaints, and associations with breasts? Well, yes, I was conscious of the role breasts played in my life, but, upon reflection, no, now I'm not booby-trapped, although I admit, I had been in the past.

On this particular day, the session started differently than most. The women went around the room doing the Daily Temperature Reading exercise, showing great appreciation for having each other in their lives. When we got to the New Information part, we shared some news.

Angela signaled she wanted to say something. She was having great difficulty beginning, searching for words. She looked around at all of us, then at the ceiling. Finally, she said, "It's New Information to you, so I've decided to tell you now." She took a breath. "I've decided to look for an intimate relationship outside my marriage. I'm looking for a love relationship. Later I will consider divorce." She became quiet, reached into her purse, took out a tissue, and began to dry the corners of her eyes.

No one said a word. I was very grateful and proud of their behavior. This was not the time to express an opinion, to lecture about family values, or even to ask for more information. Angela was in pain. She had not chosen to use the New Information part of the session appropriately since it was intended for more administrative information, but she must have been overflowing with what she wanted to tell us.

Now she took her time. She told us about the unfairness in her marriage of five years. It became a long monologue about a life that was intense, including career accomplishments, professional satisfaction, and social climbing. What had been missing for her, however, was some connection to intimacy, passion, and a basic feeling of togetherness. She reminded us that, in the past, she mentioned the heartache and loneliness she had experienced with Jim, her husband. Both were intense, opinionated, ambitious individuals. They reacted fast, sometimes without thinking through their arguments. Now, she was thinking through what she was experiencing. Angela went on to tell us about her feelings of desperation, how she thought she was not good enough for Jim.

"I've finally started to accept myself," she said. "I can see how I might even like myself. But the marriage—it is not going to work for me. Jim will never be relaxed or glad with what he has accomplished. He is so high strung and calls on me to satisfy most of his crazy needs. These needs to impress or to be approved of used to be my needs, too. But it has been two years since I've been involved in the parties and the ego boosts.

"First I lost interest in being a decoration for my husband. I became bored with being glamorous for the sake of his reputation or for his getting points with his buddies.

"I began to notice that we didn't give ourselves a chance to enjoy each other quietly, tenderly. When Beth used to tell us about the simple joys of her intimate relationship at home alone with a loving husband, I thought she was making it up. Grace used to mention her two married sons and the sweetness of their intimacies with their spouses. I would listen like she was telling us the plot to some movie script. Jane would give us legitimate tips from her parents' experiences and the way her husband and she used to be playful together. Dr. Nili commented about pleasure and its powerful effect on our well-being. I didn't want to take you seriously." She paused. "Except I know you well, and my loneliness has opened my eyes." She paused again and took a deep breath.

"Here is what is happening in our household. I want to have a child. He wants a new car. Another car with this hot look. Or get this, I'm ready for spending time together, alone. He invites three couples to spend the entire weekend. I want to make love, be with him, and spend time alone. He tells me about a new porno movie he has in the closet. In fact he brings work home and says I should have appreciated that action. After all, he could have gone to the office for the entire evening. There is much more, but I need to stop for a moment."

It was somewhat familiar to us, but Angela was also showing signs of growth. The evolution was not only in the expression of her pain. Until now, Angela usually came across as completely self-absorbed. She had represented Jim's wishes as her own. When we discussed Rosie's wish for a child, it was Angela who made a comment that she had wanted one too. But Angela had second thoughts and added that other people's experiences taught her that she might lose her figure. She also used to say that spending time alone with her husband was too restrictive. She needed social stimulation. Yet, with all the sadness she had expressed, she showed a strong wish for self-identity, a need to develop and become a separate human. Not separation, as in divorce, but as an independent soul. Now she was definitely on the road to developing a *differentiated* self.

The group showed empathy and warmth toward Angela. Each one was willing to listen and support her.

Isabel spoke first. "It's enough that you have learned to like yourself. It doesn't matter if he doesn't find you perfect, as he probably has been projecting on to you anyway." While Isabel talked, Angela appeared preoccupied and agitated.

Beth spoke next. "I'm thrilled that you wish so strongly to find intimacy and love in your life. It's time to feel loved. I'll be happy to talk more about it when you feel like it."

Angela stared into the distance. Then she put her face in both her hands. It looked like she was crying, but no sound came out.

Finally, Jane said, "I wish you would share with us what is going on with you. I see the suffering and I hear you say you want an affair. You probably have one already—do you?" She paused. "If not, is your husband having an affair?" When there was still no answer from Angela, Jane asked more forcefully, "Is he? Are you going to tell us?" Then more softly, "How long have you known about it?"

Someone in the group took a deep breath. I looked around the room. They seemed uncomfortable with this inquisition. I turned to Jane. "Let's stop this line of questioning now, okay?" Looking back, I can see that moment as an important turn of events for the group.

The feeling of confusion lingered, and I felt I had to comment further on Jane's questions, which did not reflect her typically empathetic personality. There was anger, almost indignation, in her questioning. I turned to her. She looked tired and upset. I started slowly. "What is upsetting you so?"

Jane bit her lower lip like a child. She was fidgeting a little, but did not take long to answer. "Am I going to talk in the middle of Angela's turn?" she said, almost pouting.

"Yes." The one word answer came from Angela who was sobbing quietly. Two or three women laughed nervously at the moment.

This was a therapeutic judgment call. I decided to continue with Jane. I maintained what I call my neutral-and-for-emergencies-only voice, and then said to Angela, "I'll take it from here. Wait for us a while." I looked at Jane expectantly. A little teary, she looked as if she were searching for the right words.

"I've no proof or anything to show," she began, and then she continued quietly. "I'm almost sure my husband Al is having an affair."

There was a new kind of silence—utter stillness. It was the kind of silence that was so dense because too much had to be addressed. No one could find the words to say anything. One of the women said something that sounded like she hoped it was not true. I joined in with the same wish, but one look at her and we knew that something was terribly wrong.

Grace was the first one to ask, "Are you telling us a fact—or sharing a doubt?"

No one else joined in the questioning. Moments like these are so difficult for friends and group members. We want to help but we don't want to scratch a fresh wound. Knowing that Jane must talk about it now made it easier to nudge her to "get it out."

Grace waited for an answer. She sat erect in her seat as if her whole body were saying "I'm here for you and I'm not going anywhere." Jane had no choice. Finally she gave into Grace's kindness.

"Thanks," she said. "I know I'll get through. It's just that I know it's not just in my head; it's in my insides." She put her hands on her chest and moved them down to her stomach. She left her hands there as if they were messengers of her dilemma. "I know, but I don't know how I know that I know. And it's driving me crazy. I bet I do sound insane. Sorry, Angela, I attacked you for no reason. I'm taking your turn and I have no answers."

Rosie suggested that it did make sense. And she added that this is how she felt growing up most of her life. "We are not insane, not even confused. We are being manipulated. I know. That is how I feel when I'm being lied to. Trust your feelings!"

To hear this from Rosie was a new treat. It was great hearing such a statement regarding trusting one's feelings—especially trusting the feelings of the body.

What Jane said was very serious. She had physical sensations that gave her information. This knowledge was transmitted to her brain. She was not paranoid. She didn't invent this information, but she somehow felt it.

In several situations, I have treated women who one day simply knew about their husbands' infidelities without having any physical evidence. In Jane's case, however, she had picked up on behavior that was especially uncomfortable for her. For example, her husband's dramatic change in how he related toward her. For most of their twenty-seven years of marriage, they had what she termed "pleasant, very predictable, once-a-week sexual contact." In the last three months, though, the contrast was so exciting and zestful that it often left her speechless. He had shown an increased sexual appetite for a few days at a time, then sudden total disinterest for several weeks. The days of sexual interest were intense and passionate. It was accompanied by deep discussions that they had never experienced before. Not being a suspicious person, Jane thought that her menopause was contributing to this new sexual energy.

She, in fact, did what many women, especially older ones, do in such situations. She took on total responsibility for the behavior. Jane was only fifty-five years old, but she looked slightly older than her age due to her more-salt-than-pepper hair. In some ways, she was also of her mother's generation. Educated as a legal secretary, she originally had no plans to make it a career, but, being extremely good at her job, she had become the administrator of a law firm where she was responsible for the work of the legal secretaries and office staff. She often trained the new attorneys in the ways of the courts.

She was also quite serene and comfortable in her friendship with Al. Now she had a strong need to tell us all about her devastating news. And so she did. We encouraged her to talk more and express the many different emotions she had simmering inside her for the past few weeks.

The way Jane's conflict came out was typical to our group work. When Angela mentioned suspicions of her husband's affair, it triggered Jane's pain. Jane found herself, for once, with no control over herself, and her outburst sounded as if she were angry with Angela. In reality, Jane was simply free-associating and projecting. This is very common practice in group process. The members of the group have deep respect for that kind of projection, and they know this is an opportunity for effective work.

Jane, however, really did not get any advice from us. It was an opportunity for her to vent weeks of impressions, thoughts, suspicion, and agony. What she got from the group this time was sympathy and understanding. In the next few weeks, though, she would return to her concerns. The novelty—the shock—was over, and Jane would learn to say what it was she wanted. This is a tough lesson for people: to dare to speak for oneself.

Angela stayed present all during Jane's "interruption." I watched how Katherine touched her shoulder a few times through Jane's confession. I also noticed that Isabel had handed tissues first to Jane, then Angela, finally leaving the box on Angela's lap. I noticed that Lisa giggled at the progress of the tissues and the box. The tissue box that week happened to be decorated with a painting. It traveled constantly throughout the session.

Grace, I noticed, was uncomfortable with Jane's report. The women had been close to each other since the inception of the group. Grace looked at Jane, and then looked at the floor and back again at Jane. Grace made no eye contact with me, however, clearly signaling she was not prepared to talk now. In most situations like this, I would have invited Grace to talk to us.

Today we had an agenda built in. I asked Grace how she was doing. She smiled at me and finally said, "I've had some better days; thanks, I'm fine." In group work these were code words—translation: I feel lousy; however, today I'm not ready to share. Leave me alone now; go climb another tree. (This is not an exact science, however, so I did check with her the following week. Yes, she was annoyed with Jane. She was afraid Jane would invent a story about Al that was off the mark and might be in danger of eventually losing him. Did it happen to someone she knew? Yes, to her daughter Amy, not long ago. Did it happen to anyone else? Yes, to her.)

Angela, in her tears, let the process continue. She had learned to trust us. And now we focused back on her.

She had stopped crying and was ready to talk about her feelings. To find out more about the directions that Angela wanted to go, one needed only to watch her body language. She took the tissue box in both hands and slowly put it on the floor far from her. This symbolic body language, graceful in its movements, said to us I am done crying. I'm here to work!

We were ready for her, I thought. I was dead wrong. True, Angela was about to work, but I really didn't anticipate her next revelation. She told us again about her feelings of being unloved. It sounded like she was telling us the same material over again, like many of us do, in order to make sure it was truly understood. This time, however, she took us for a spin. She told about Jim's treatment of her that was different from what she had mentioned before.

By my basic norms of aesthetics, attractiveness, and beauty, Angela was definitely what anyone would call drop-dead gorgeous. No aging process or lack of fashion accessories could diminish her classic beauty. Yet, she didn't know that she was that beautiful.

She came out of her self-pity mode and shared some deeper things. Apparently, their relationship had gotten progressively worse. Jim used to call her demeaning names or raise his voice, but moments later he would get sexually turned on and she would forget his outbursts and forgive him and was ravished in his passion. Angela actually enjoyed all of this with Jim. She had not paid attention to the fact that he was intensifying the name calling and ordering her around in close association with these sexual activities. In many instances, Jim was right in line with her fantasies.

He would mention names of other models they had both personally known and compare Angela's body parts to those of the other females. He emphasized the fact that a friend's body was more curvaceous and better built in a language that was unkind and degrading.

She told of being shamed as if she were deformed and unfit to be a woman. Her voice was calm; she was determined to tell us the entire story. I remember thinking that her posture, her tone of voice, did not match the content of this particular narrative. She didn't seem to be personally involved. What was missing was the pain, the expressions of shame she was alluding to. But I did not say this out loud, trusting the therapeutic process. It paid off.

Angela began to explain what she had been through. First it was a sexual turn-on, which she interpreted as being wanted. Next, the humiliation and the passionate sexual encounters, which she thought were expressions of love and forgiveness. The parts about being compared to others were familiar aspects from her past, which Angela agreed with. She actually went along and validated her husband's descriptions of her underdeveloped body. This was the standard of beauty she had perceived for herself.

Suddenly, her tone of voice changed. She burst out sobbing and her entire body shook.

For a whole minute she cried, then stopped and looked at me saying, "I owe it to myself to tell you the truth. I should have done this kind of work a few weeks back when you suggested it. I'm ready now. Here it is." She gulped air. "Two years ago I had my breasts done. I have implants, too. My breasts are doubled from their original size. I was kind of small to begin with, and I guess my breasts were really fine for what I needed for my modeling career. I thought I liked my boobs and if I got old and saggy, I could fix them in the future. But can you imagine the surgery, the fear of the outcome? How stupid can one be?" She paused.

"You know how much I like to wear tailored jackets; you've seen me in them every meeting. I like especially the double-breasted ones. So I called my new boobs 'double breasts' because they are. Sometimes I'm not sure about my breasts any more. I don't know if you've noticed but I would never wear a low cut top or one that is too tight. I'm still trying to decide if I like them—my breasts, I mean. It's confusing and therefore hard to tell if I like them. Jim wanted big breasts so much, so very much. It was an obsession of his that I couldn't figure out. I called them 'The Replacements.' They stand in for what my normal body used to be. Actually, he was sexually turned on for a long time. He still likes my breasts, I think, but now he wants me to reshape my thighs with liposuction. I don't know about that. I don't think I want to go through with this. I think I want to punch his face out." Angela stopped.

The room was spinning. Every single person had something to say—to Angela, to me, probably to Jim. The energy in the room was electric. Questions, associations, remarks, passing the tissue box, empathy, and more questions.

Naomi Wolf, in her bestseller *The Beauty Myth,* said it so well:

> When men are more aroused by symbols of sexuality than by the sexuality of women themselves, they are fetishists. Fetishism treats a part as if it were the whole; men who choose a lover on the basis of her 'beauty' alone are treating the woman as a fetish—that is, treating a part of her, her visual image, not even her skin, as if it were her sexual self. Freud suggested that the fetish is a talisman against the failure to perform.

We ended this session hugging, crying, and laughing. Angela was back in control. On the way out of the office, I watched her bend over and pick up the tissue box from the floor. She looked at the box and smiled. This was the tissue box with a picture of the Mona Lisa painted on it. Angela picked up one tissue. "One for the road," she said and disappeared into the cool night. The tissue box was empty.

When I arrived home that night, I reached for some books I had left in the trunk of my car. In the darkness of the parking lot, I pulled out an unfamiliar packet. As I uncovered it, I had a good laugh. It was a large commercial size carton full of tissue boxes from Costco. One should be prepared at all times.

Chapter Seven

The BREAST Dialogues

Two Days Later

Feminine armor is never metal or muscle but, paradoxically, an exaggeration of physical vulnerability that is reassuring (unthreatening) to men.

—from Femininity, by Susan Brownmiller

Although our breasts do shape our lives, the essential part of who we are is much deeper than that. What I find beautiful is strength, independence, intelligence—qualities that don't come from perky breasts and an unlined face, but from an attitude that can't help but shine through.

—from Breasts, by Meema Spadola

THE "DOUBLE-BREASTS" EPISODE WAS ONE OF THE MAJOR EVENTS in our group's emotional history. The reactions were intense and varied, ranging from empathy to anger, admiration, identification, envy, humiliation, and betrayal. It is difficult to digest the concept of volunteering to go through a surgical procedure like implants, and actually not wanting it for yourself. Or not knowing if it was your wish or his command.

Actually, I had been thinking about Angela's predicament a few times that week. On Friday afternoon, I caught myself thinking about her again.

I get myself into this habit known as "occupational therapy." Or as my late grandmother used to say, go make yourself useful! While doing something with my hands, which is familiar, purposeful, productive, and pleasant, I'm also making sure that my mind is free to wander. That Friday, I was preparing for the Sabbath meal. I chose to prepare the recipes that I know by heart. Nothing I made that day was new or complicated. I had a need for simplicity so my mind could rest. The meal's design was taking shape: a little chicken soup, some noodles, and the little dish of carrots that my mom still makes on holidays, a little bit of this and that, and I was busy for the next two hours.

Personally, I prefer to make the soup first so its aroma spreads throughout the kitchen and turns my house into a home in one whiff. I stood over the sink, washing all of these delectably perfect vegetables, admiring their colors, their firmness, their amazing nutritional value, and especially their variety.

This is my appreciation ritual. I find myself doing this every time I make my version of this semitraditional chicken soup. I know that I am killing off most of the nutritional value by cooking the vegetables. On this occasion, however, as soon as I'd washed each separate vegetable, I noticed that the radio was playing a love song. I was also aware of my muscles relaxing as they usually do after a workout session. I took an inventory of my body and I realized I could not relax my neck. Who's my pain in the neck, I thought?

I was not aware of when Angela entered my thoughts. She was watching my hands and my rhythmic movements to the music, and was waiting to be addressed. In reality, I was in the kitchen cooking. In my imagination, I had a guest visitor. This is not unusual when you have unfinished emotional business. Angela had been intensely on my mind. So I sat her down and we had a drink of water.

Angela retold the agonizing relationship story she told the group. Now, though, I had time to reflect. I had just put a big pot on the stove, half-filled with salted water. On the cutting board were four pieces of skinless, boneless chicken breasts ready to be trimmed of fat. Usually I enjoy this process of taking care of my family's nutrition. I had discovered over the years that doing the minute stuff gave me more pleasure than obtaining a result. And here at home, indulging in the "doing," I was removed enough from the office to see a bigger clinical picture, not just the pain.

Perfect timing, I thought to myself. Here I am with my four chicken breasts imagining talking to Angela about her four. I smiled. So is this what they call irony?

For the soup, cutting up the ingredients makes a difference. While the chicken breasts are cooking, I customarily cut a few potatoes, carrots, celery, and any green vegetables I have into small cubes.

Once I skim the foamy froth from the top layer of boiling water, the pot is ready for the vegetables. I add more water to cover them. Now, for my secret ingredients. Today, they're brussels sprouts. The aroma, the taste, the colors are heaven on earth. When the soup is half done, I put in some fresh parsley and a bunch of fresh dill. Then season to taste.

The ritual of washing and cutting vegetables was almost finished by the time I recalled Angela's entire story. I was sad and disturbed. I left the chicken and veggies simmering and went to sit in my library. Angela was with me, in my head, waiting. As I moved some books and papers around and got settled to read, I recognized that I had seen her predicament before, especially with women. I had treated a few couples with similar dynamics. I was not thinking of a particular case, but it's the script, the story line, and the underlying philosophy of life that made it all so helpless. Here is what I mean: The female in the marriage of equally successful partners is existing in two emotional spheres. In her one reality, she is highly functioning as an independent professional. In the other reality, she is a devoted wife who is capable of losing her integrity and identifying with her husband's wishes, even when it means altering a part of her body. At the time, she was convinced that his wishes were her wishes, too.

Symbolically, Angela represents many modern women. After all, she has an unusual collection of external characteristics and internal traits. Angela is feminine, successful, sexy, intuitive, professional, helpful, resourceful, focused, and aware. It has been a fantastic era in which to be a talented woman! She is also a woman of color and the commercial demand for professional models with her skin tone and physical attributes is great.

And then there are these ambivalent components inherit in her personality. Since her infancy, she was sensitive and aware, therefore she also heard and internalized many expectations, criticisms, and projections. On several occasions, girls take in these messages and create an impossible ideal. That process of creating an often unobtainable ideal may be damaging to one of the most precious, wholesome parts of our personality: our self-image.

I view Angela as an explicit example of femininity today and Jim as the representation of our culture, in a general sense. His pressures on his wife to compete in areas that she had no desire to participate in made him transparent to us. She was comfortable with her breast size. After all, in her case, as a professional model she had the exact body type for the job. The amazing part was that she was not good enough, and not because she had small breasts or lack of feminine charm. It was because Jim had not felt virile, manly enough in his own image of himself. It was obvious how Angela had no chance to be her own fully developed, evolved person living in her present environment. Her femininity was too much in his face, if you will. Therefore, he felt that his inadequacies had been magnified, and he came to a kind of boiling point. The culture, depicted as Jim, had trapped Angela, symbol of femininity, into a corner. That is a dangerous and lonely place for women. As we have already seen, it is only a matter of time before an eruption occurs.

Sometimes knowledge acquired from books can be as nurturing as chicken soup to the body and soul. Today I needed both the soup and the knowledge. The book I wanted to refer to explained Jim's behavior and attitude. It even shed some light on Angela's pain.

In the book *Observing the Erotic Imagination* by Robert J. Stoller, M.D., Jim is easily identified with the main description of a patient whose perception of relationships, especially intimacy, is twisted and entangled in some infantile needs. This person has been severely hurt in his childhood, emotionally or physically or both. As a result, he has unconsciously devised a psychological story, a script, to escape the remembrance of the traumatic pain of the past. Dr. Stoller calls this behavior a perversion. At the beginning of the book, he explains that the concept of perversion means the desire to sin, to hurt, to be cruel is the mechanism of being turned-on. The person that will be harmed is viewed as the *sex-object*.

I recalled the first group meetings when we each got to tell about ourselves including our personal, intimate love lives. Angela was the one who presented herself as having an unexpectedly passionate and excitable sex life with her husband. She was surprised about this, since her own level of sexual need, she confessed, was pretty low.

Jim was the only one, thus far, who could wake in her such sexual excitement. It was not about their mutual attraction to each other. It was about what she called "The Jim Show": his body, his creativity, his pleasuring himself, and last but not least, his audience. However, Angela had to actively participate in many of his fantasies, his dramatizations to get her sexual highs. His creativity had no bounds; he was a natural producer and director of all of their sexual games.

The group had listened with almost no verbal reactions. Since it was still early in our sessions, some were shy, some intimidated, and others were simply speechless. I think that it was only Katherine who found it interesting and fun. Lisa, Beth, and Isabel were impressed with how romantic it all sounded. Jane said something to the effect that Angela should write a book.

Now I observed that Angela had volunteered thus far only the parts about the amusement and creativity. It has been almost one year since she started to open up. Carefully, one glimpse at a time, the picture of her shame and humiliation had finally unraveled. For reasons that were unfolding, Angela chose to tell us just a sketchy version of her reality. The group accepted and admired her sexual stories. Angela was by far, it appeared, the most erotically adventurous one among these women, and the group benefited tremendously from Angela's sharing, since we had a glimpse beyond the standardized context of the understanding of human sexuality. Dr. Stoller writes:

> It is not easy to get a safe and loving intimacy by means of anger and the desire to harm. How can you reach another person if you transform him or her, by means of your scripts, into something he or she is not, something less than full person-hood? Even a pornographer's seemingly trivial airbrush removes the truth, the little blemishes that are unbearable, unaesthetic.

> This is dehumanization. With it, because we cannot stand the revelations of intimacy, we deprive others of their fullness. We see them only as members of classes or as possessors of selected parts or qualities only. We anato-

mize them. And if even that is too intimate, we turn from humans to inanimate objects, such as garments, granting them a certain amount of humanness while not needing humans. By doing this in fantasy, for a moment, as long as we can write, direct, and produce the show, we avoid anxiety or, even worse, despair.

I have emphasized how one dehumanizes his objects in order to feel safe enough to get excited. There is a price: doing so dehumanizes the dehumanizer and that knowledge is not always unconscious.

The trauma in each perversion script—whether the story is told as a daydream, pornography, or performance in reality—is converted to triumph. The attackers of earlier times are defeated, undone, and unable to persist in their attack. Now, each new episode of trauma is constructed so that the victim is not defeated, though the experience is carried out using the same essential that had earlier led to the disaster. Now the victim is the victor and the trauma a triumph, the crazy optimism of full erection. If the story is well constructed, one feels guiltless and without anxiety. In this brilliant replay lies the idea that the old attackers have been thwarted and thereby humiliated; and humiliation is the fundamental experience that is exchanged in these episodes. By humiliating, one gets revenge for having been humiliated.

I'd never met Jim in person, yet reading these painful lines in the book made me aware that I had known his symptoms and behaviors well. I've met a few Jim-like people in my life, some professionally and some socially. In my many years of practicing psychotherapy, I've observed a great deal along the range of human behaviors. At this stage, there are no more surprises about perversions and bizarre acts.

The more eccentric or off-center the act and the more twisting of the soul and mind, the greater the human suffering it represents.

In spite of the lack of specific information about his childhood, Jim's personality was coming more into focus. I was not sure about the abuse or punishment he had received as a child. There was no biological father around. We did hear some evidence of two stepfathers who were alcoholics and a mother who could have been. The mother had multiple boyfriends who moved in and lived with the family. There was, however, no true fathering. His behavior, demeanor, and attitude tell me of a child subjected to shame, humiliation, and emotional abuse. I continued to read Dr. Stoller's book; it was as if he were analyzing Jim himself:

> The exhibitionist knows he was humiliated, knows it was traumatic, knows it was a repetition, knows he is vulnerable to that humiliation, knows that in the humiliating attack on him are statements about himself he has always known, knows he wants revenge, knows he must pick strangers, knows the social rumpus is important. He knows so much. His aesthetic task is to keep knowing what he knows and yet to not know. (Freud called this 'splitting.') So then we get mysteries and secrets and illusions and scripts. We get details that are thrown in not by chance but because they speak. And we get risks that are pseudo-risks. The actor knows that.

> We really do know that perversion is theater. If there were no mystery, secrets, and illusions, there would be— God forbid—insight. For perversion, insight is the death of excitement. It would require one to come to terms with the trauma and develop the ability to enjoy intimacy with someone else rather than deny it with a manic outburst, the perversion.

I haven't yet mentioned one of the chief factors in my symbolic chicken breast soup. I view Angela as a pretty assertive woman when it comes to promoting her career, negotiating a contract, or initiating a deal. She is good. She has also reported to the group that she has assisted several friends, especially young black models, in launching their modeling careers. She knows how to make it in a tough, competitive world. Where are her powers when it comes to fighting for her integrity, her femininity, her soul? To what extent has she been booby-trapped?

Remember the session when she discussed her preoccupation with body parts, practicing her modeling in front of her father, using parts of herself to show and exhibit the things she liked? Well, what do we have here but the perfect counterpart to Jim, the humiliator. Angela, the one who "needed" to be humiliated. The historical piece about using her "parts" was clinically fascinating. She did this herself by only appreciating one functioning part of herself at a time, and only when that part was excelling at its performance. And as if by magic, she had found her match in Jim who would cut her to pieces using criticisms, profanities, put-downs, and surgical procedures.

I sat there thinking when the aroma of the cooked chicken soup engulfed me. The cutting and dicing of my beautiful veggies, boiling them, wasting their original nutritional value, looked to me now more wasteful than ever.

There is a theory that speaks directly to the subject of men humiliating others, especially women. According to Dr. Stoller, this theory shows how, in some cases, men focus only on certain anatomic parts or partial aspects of the personality of women. They ignore the fact that women are human.

Angela was apparently familiar with that feeling of being ignored as a whole person; instead, she was appreciated for the ability to act as an object. She found a partner who could provoke that very dynamic in her, keeping her busy and totally immersed in the state of mind of being a collection of adored parts. She needed it, too, for most of her life—until now.

Angela had grown. We watched her taking in the feedback she was getting from us. She was struggling about being appreciated as a kind and generous whole person, the one she had never recognized herself to be. She began opening up to us, developing trust in her own judgment in relationships. Lately, as a result of the wakening of her self-worth, she was finally becoming frustrated with a lack of intimacy in her marriage.

The first time she talked about that, the group could not clearly follow her line of thinking. The portrayal that she presented about herself and Jim was just too perfect. They were glamorous, social, media animals. Their pictures were often published in the pages of popular magazines and catalogues. They were a hot couple.

But the marriage had no emotional nurturing. Their commitment was not about sharing pleasure, support, and intimacy. It was about looking good. All these years of sharing the social excitement made them an icon among their peers, but they had not learned to be with each other as basic humans in an intimate relationship. The group was aware of their public personae, but they also wanted this fairy tale marriage to be emotionally satisfying.

Nurturing is what our society sees today through the analogy of chicken soup. It is the healer to the body and the soul. That was my unconscious message to Angela. I had no idea this message was cooking inside me the entire time.

Before the group left that last historical session, we experienced some comic relief. Angela, who felt elation from unloading her secret and sharing her heavy heart, turned to the group at the end of the meeting and said, "If my breasts could talk, they would asked to be left alone already…"

The group reacted with loud laughter. Maybe more laughter than warranted. The relief was welcomed. Tina, who is always a step ahead, jumped from her seat, laughing. "My breasts are talking, but no one is listening. They want an appointment with Lisa's breasts to discuss some urgent matters." Tina looked sideways to Lisa with that spark in her eyes.

Lisa does not need any encouragement when it comes to talk about breasts. She responded immediately. "You mean we'll have a dialogue, right? I'll go for that. If the vagina can monologue, our breasts should dialogue! Whose breasts are in for that?"

Beth reacted, "The roaring of laughter is music to my ears. The content is original and fresh. I like that idea. My breasts will love to dialogue with sisters' breasts. My breasts will recite poetry about femininity and beauty."

Pat was waving her hands in the air saying, "My breasts will not carry a dialogue with the rest of you. They are too busy talking between them. They are arguing who is the favorite one. The left one just said 'she loves you more' while the right one said 'no way, she loves you more—I saw it this morning when she touched you!' I am a walking-talking war zone." She was smiling, but her message sure came through.

Grace did not participate until Angela nudged her a little. "Alright, I'll tell all. They always ask for air and space. They are always too hot in there and they say they are too crowded. Complaints, complaints. I wish they'd stop. I've never heard a good word from them. I get no respect from my breasts."

These breast dialogues continued for a while.

At the next session, Angela said she had learned much from her group work. She had arranged for Jim and her to attend a P.A.I.R.S. seminar for intimacy skills. He had actually heard her cry of loneliness and heartache in the marriage. Their journey to an intimate relationship was about to begin.

Chapter Eight

It's Not Nice to FOOL Mother Nature!

The Following Week

The newest porn magazine is Perfect 10. It is the world's first silicone-free pornography, whose models are guaranteed by its publishers to boast only the real thing.

—from *Survival of the Prettiest,*
    by Nancy Etcoff

For better or for worse, bigger or smaller, in sickness and in health, breasts are wedded to our bodies and, in the best of circumstances, can offer us both pleasure and power.

—from *A History of the Breast,*
    by Marilyn Yalom

THE VERY NEXT GROUP MEETING WAS CHARACTERIZED BY personal reactions to what Angela had confessed. The comments ranged from empathy to envy to anger and back.

Grace contributed by saying that, after a few days' thinking about it, the shock had worn off. "If this doesn't sound like the Chinese feet wrap," she said, "I don't know what does."

I held my breath and thought how creative and profound this analogy was. A predictable group reaction, however, came quickly.

Lisa, who never misses a beat but whose knowledge of other cultures was missing, asked, "What about those feet?" Isabel asked Lisa to relax, and there was now an opening for some educational, anthropological, and even inspirational conversation. As usual, they all wanted to talk and share. Lisa's curiosity and innocence provoked the mother, teacher, and caretaker in all of us.

The analogy of the breast implants to wrapping Chinese girls' feet made for a riveting moment. Jane recalled a movie she had seen in which there were women with bound feet. Rosie remembered having written a paper once on the subject. She could not wait to tell us about it. She even had a new kind of "shine" about her. Rosie told us about the practice that had begun in the Sung Dynasty, from 960–976 A.D., in China. A prince started binding the feet of girls because he thought the daintiness of his imperial concubines' feet were lovely. By the twelfth century, the practice was widespread and more severe: girls' feet were bound so tightly, they were unable to dance and had difficulty walking.

Thus, traditional Chinese values for over 1,000 years dictated that the feet of young girls should be bound to keep them small. "Lily feet," as they were called, were thought to be beautiful and a symbol of gentility and high class. Although the term sounded harmless, the practice was extremely cruel. It began when a girl was between the ages of three and eleven years old. First her foot was washed in hot water and massaged. Then the child's toes were turned under and pressed against the bottom of her foot. The arches were broken, and a long narrow cotton bandage was tightly wound around the foot from the toes to the ankle to hold the toes in place.

After two to three years, a girl's feet actually shrunk until they could fit into shoes just three inches long. This resulted in feet that were highly deformed and unbearably painful to walk on. Sometimes the toes even fell off because blood could no longer reach them. Besides identifying women of gentility or high class, foot binding prevented women from "wandering." These women had to walk with tiny, mincing steps and could stand only with great difficulty.

Some, however, adapted. The father of a friend of mine, who grew up in China as the son of missionaries, had an amah—or Chinese nurse—whose feet had been bound as a little girl. My friend's father thought this gave him an advantage in evading her when he had been naughty. He was wrong. "She could really move on her heels," he told my friend, "when she wanted to catch me."

Tiny three-inch-long shoes called "lotus shoes" were made of silk and beautifully embroidered. In upper classes in China, a good marriage would be impossible to arrange if the girl had "big ugly feet." The practice of foot binding continued in China for more than 1,000 years until the Manchu Dynasty was toppled in 1911 and the new republic was formed. At that point, foot binding was outlawed.

Some Chinese women and girls who came to California had their feet bound as small children in China. They had to spend their lives with the useless feet. Many of them, however, did manage to walk and could do light household tasks and cooking. Sometimes the young girls would have the bindings removed and often their feet would grow enough to permit normal walking.

Rosie, with a painful expression on her face, finished reporting and put her papers down. The response of the group was tremendous. Some were crying; some looked sad. Beth made a statement about how fortunate we are to be living in a free country. Jane said that every time she thought of such abuses, her heart went out to the women who had to endure them, especially the little girls. Only Tina attempted humor, although it seemed to mask her anguish: "I'll never say that my feet are killing me again!"

We learned from Rosie that she had found the information on the Internet, a feat in itself since Rosie considered herself computer illiterate. This project, understandably, had become a source of pride for her.

Katherine also told us about a study conducted by medical professors at the University of California–San Francisco. They had researched hundreds of Chinese women between the ages of seventy and eighty. They learned that more than 38 percent of the women had bound-foot deformities. They also found that those with bound feet were more likely to have fallen during the previous years than women with normal feet. These women were also less able to rise from a chair without assistance. Katherine pointed out they also had difficulty squatting, an ability that was particularly important to going to the toilet and performing other daily activities in China. Katherine stated that studies show how deformities of foot binding remain as a cause of disability in elderly Chinese women.

Grace passed around a picture she had found in an anthropological magazine—a scary sight. Lisa went on about the poor little girls, their tiny feet and baby-like toes, "How do they walk?"

Tina gave a wry chuckle, "Very slowly." Then she asked Lisa, "How come you are so intense about this topic?"

"I am beauty conscious, I guess," Lisa said. "In any case, I don't tolerate this barbaric behavior very well. It is ugly."

"Look, Lisa," Beth said. "No matter where you are, beauty is a subjective experience. Twiggy, the 1960s skinny super-model from Britain would not have a chance in the Middle East where Dr. Nili was raised. On the other hand, here large breasts were totally unnecessary one hundred years ago. Some tribes even today don't notice women's breasts as a body part worth mentioning or even justifying in covering up. The breasts are just there for a biological purpose, not as something women need to compete over."

Lisa tried to argue, "But it's about beauty and femininity..."

"This is *not* about beauty," Beth continued. "You've got it all wrong if that's what you think. It's about one superior exercising his power over someone else. Those girls became mothers and saw the small, broken up feet of their daughters as an expression of tradition. Over the years, feet-binding became the standard of feminine beauty among Chinese aristocracy. The final product was the small feet, which became acceptable as feminine and attractive in that culture. If you consider the binding of the feet as a political act, you can appreciate how the use of power, in this case, can be abusive."

Beth voice rose. The other women looked at each other, understanding her passion. As she had on numerous occasions, Beth could make a roomful of intelligent women feel like schoolgirls. Sometimes she did this by showing her vast knowledge of a subject, but most of the time it was her tone: authoritative, no-nonsense, and know-it-all. Beth was fully aware of this ability and told us that her husband has reacted as strongly to her as some of the women in the group do. She looked around and made a quick note of how she was lecturing again.

Rosie felt bewildered from the conversation. She looked up to Beth, her admiration reflected in her voice. "So much power and control over nature. A few people at the top of the hierarchy, like an emperor, can really change what was once perfectly normal," she said.

"It's not nice to fool Mother Nature," Beth chose a phrase from an old TV commercial, trying to sound playful after her "lecture."

There was surprise on their faces and they laughed.

Grace made the point about causing so much pain to children. She was obviously upset. "I just want to say this. In my experience as a social worker I thought I'd seen it all, from overly spoiled children to burning their little bodies alive." She paused and then said, "I should've been desensitized by now to the capacity that humans have for abusing others who pose no threat to them. I've always been moved by this period in human history, especially the inhuman treatment of girls. I hope women everywhere will remember never to let anyone manipulate, change, or deform their bodies like that."

Katherine needed to speak. "Not just young girls, Grace. Let's be fair here. What about the eight-day-old Jewish male baby who undergoes circumcision, not just then but now? This is another way to use the body, this time not for beauty but for religious purposes."

Pat's voice was soft, as if she were still thinking. "Looks like the extreme measures were not for beauty only, but to identify certain groups or tribes—the need to be the same so you can belong to them."

The subject matter had changed from attempts at beautifying oneself to the control society has over us.

Katherine cleared her throat. "Before we hook into the religious aspect, though, it's wise to note that circumcision of males is a routine procedure in the U.S." She looked around apologetically. "I'm sorry to throw in some statistics here, but I think it's necessary that we know the facts before we go into other aspects." Getting no objection, she continued.

"The trend toward circumcision started only toward the second half of the twentieth century. In fact, only 10 to 15 percent of men throughout the world are circumcised, even now." Seeing some raised eyebrows, she added, "You know, there has always been a body of knowledge that opposes circumcision."

Pat said, "I can't remember whether it was the Greeks or the Romans who passed a law against it. And later on, the Catholic Church did so as well. It would be interesting to find out how it became so pervasive in the States since this is not the norm among European boys."

Beth had the information to complete the picture. "Remember in your history classes?" she said. "Well, during the masturbation hysteria that occurred in the Victorian Era, some American doctors circumcised boys as punishment for masturbation. Victorian doctors soon claimed that circumcision cured disorders such as epilepsy, tuberculosis, insanity, and so many others. No procedure in the history of medicine has been claimed to cure and prevent more diseases than circumcision did. As late as the 1970s, leading American medical textbooks still advocated routine circumcision as a way to prevent masturbation. The wide practice of circumcision spread at the same time breast-feeding was discouraged and natural birth became medicalized." Beth took a deep breath and turned to Katherine as if seeking support.

Katherine did not disappoint her. "Good job, Beth!"

My group therapy had taken another turn and become a sincere study group of anthropology. The members closely examined other cultures that had permanently modified the human form. The information was amazing. It had become clearer and clearer how a nation or a chosen group delivered their perfectly shaped-by-nature bodies to be manipulated for the sake of identity and belonging to a tribe, class, or religion.

At this point, Jane stepped forward to educate us. She came to the next session ready for show and tell. She opened a Bible to the Old Testament and read from what I gathered was a quotation from Genesis 17:10-12:

> This shall be the covenant that you shall keep between Me and you and your children after you: you shall circumcise all males. And you shall circumcise the flesh of your foreskin, and this shall be the sign of the covenant between Me and you. And at eight days old you shall circumcise all males for all generations.

Jane explained how circumcision had been started 3,800 years ago by Abraham, who had performed it on himself. Later, when his son Isaac was born, Abraham had circumcised him on the eighth day after his birth. Since then, circumcision must be performed on all Jewish baby boys on their eighth day. Jane tried hard to be objective, but her voice carried another message. I could tell from her efforts to simply report the history that she had an appreciation for the tradition. She sounded, however, uncomfortable retelling the part about an infant being cut at only eight days old.

Katherine reassured her. She also heard the ambivalence in Jane's voice. Katherine's empathy was right on target and she promoted a discussion about the power of religious rituals in our life. The opinions flooded in. Some of us could not bear the cruelty to children, others talked about the control society exercises on humans, still others wanted more information. Why do it on the eighth day?

It was Grace who surprised the group by offering an explanation from her studies of the Kabala, Jewish mysticism. "Any given eight days on the calendar will always include at least one Sabbath," she said. "That day corresponds with the number seven, which represents the natural order of the world. Thus circumcision represents something that is higher than nature." Grace became silent after her attempt to explain this reason for circumcision. It appeared that she was thinking it over. Finally, she shared with us that she had never questioned the rationale of this tradition until today.

"I'm going to think about this more," Grace said. "All of a sudden, after hearing again the story about the Chinese lily feet, my eyes have opened. I have become more aware. I want to take a second look at what I used to appreciate as tradition."

"All members pay the price of entry into a higher status or culture," Beth said. "You see, their elders did not consider this an abuse, nor did they regard the beauty or fashion aspects of it. It was a way to control the masses using all the means available."

Jane rejoined the conversation. She said, "What I think I hear you saying is that authorities do these cruel procedures because they can. I mean, no one objects. Over the years the procedure becomes tradition and no one questions the authorities."

"I can't help but think about another kind of circumcision," said Pat. "Not the traditional Jewish kind and not the reaction to masturbation in the Victorian era. I'm talking about female circumcision." Some of the women held their breath as she said those words. Most had never talked about it. Some had known a few facts but wanted to dismiss the reality of it.

Historically, female circumcision began in northeastern Africa as a ritual; by means of Islam, it spread westward through parts of northern Africa and into the Middle East. Pat gave some statistics that made our skin crawl. It has been estimated that between 80 million to 100 million women have been circumcised. They represent 50 percent to 90 percent of Egyptian women, 90 percent of Sudanese women, and almost 100 percent of Somali and Djibouti women.

The Western world was not ignored, especially during the Victorian era. There were many women who had clitorectomies performed on them because of what men thought was a tendency toward nymphomania. Nymphomania was diagnosed for women who showed an interest in sex. The removal of the clitoris was considered a method of ensuring that a woman would not masturbate or enjoy sex. This procedure was performed well into this century in America as a medical practice. The Western world is not so different from Africa and the Middle East in the traditional treatment of women's sexuality.

The women in the group were upset and obviously emotionally moved by the information provided. A long discussion about the control and slavery still being practiced on humans in our "enlightened" world followed.

Jane reiterated her theory about the few who manipulate the bodies of others simply because they can do it. Most of the group agreed.

When I experienced the tremendous interest these women had about culture dictating over autonomy and anatomy, I wanted to brush up on my education. I called one of my dearest friends and asked her to spend a day with me, filling in the many blanks in my knowledge. Abigail Lubliner is one of the most fascinating women I've ever known. She's an anthropologist who also collects ritualistic arts and crafts from the most primitive cultures. I'd joined her years ago on an anthropological expedition into the rainforest of Borneo. I watched her interacting with the natives and finding out about short cuts through the jungle. I also observed, with admiration, how she prepared for an expedition, searching out and collecting the latest texts on her destinations.

Spending a day with my dear friend Abigail was for me as stimulating as attending the most fascinating seminar on human behavior. Spending a full month with her on an expedition could compare to a year of study at a university. I feel fortunate to have her as a friend.

Abigail traveled to Thailand a few times over the past few years. On one of those trips, she visited a certain tribe with one of the cruelest behaviors toward women any civilization has ever encountered. When Abigail told me about the tribe, she pulled out photographs she had taken and a few postcards. She placed them on the table where we were having lunch. Listening to her, I lost my appetite, and signaled the waiter to remove my plate. The photos consisted of a group of eight women sitting on the porch of a house. They looked exotic with Far Eastern facial features and long, raven black, straight hair. They were all sitting very erect, and at first glance they seemed peaceful and rather elegant. As I studied the photos, I realized that each one of them had golden rings around her neck. Upon further examination, I noticed something odd about their postures.

Abigail took the photos in her hands and let out a sigh. She put her hand over mine, as if to comfort me for what I was about to hear. It was completely intuitive on her part. She was right. I needed it. Then she told me.

"A few months ago, I visited Thailand for the third time. This time I explored the northern part of the country, the Karen village of the Thai Hill tribe to be exact. I saw these women sitting on the porch exactly like in this photo. I spent a few days among them learning about their special circumstances. Here is what I've learned. Before they are six years old, all the girls in the village are made to wear a set of brass rings that rest around their necks. The rings are heavy and they fit tightly from the shoulders to the top of the neck, right under the chin."

Abigail stooped, reached into her bag, and pulled out an object. "Here, weigh this." I looked at the object. It was a small spiral ring. "It's not light, is it?" she said. No, I shook my head. "Well," she continued, "we commonly think the rings elongate the neck. But actually they push the ribs down so there is an illusion of a long neck. These women are called 'giraffe women' by the neighboring villagers. The women can never remove the brass rings. They sleep with their necks erect. They cannot even turn their heads."

Abigail took the brass ring back and held it above the table with both of her hands. "It looks like the rings are resting on the collarbone," she said, "but actually they rest directly on the ribs. Their ribs are constantly under pressure. Since the ribs are connected to the vertebrae by a hinge joint, they grow down, and the brass rings slide deeper into the ribs. Every time a spiral ring drops deeper into the shoulders, it becomes too short and loose. Then more brass rings are added, so the new set of rings is heavier. Thus, the entire cylinder of brass rings begins to push down the ribs even more. It's the brass rings that hold the neck up. The muscles lose their tone and finally deteriorate completely."

Abigail stopped talking and reached for a glass of water, her eyes had welled up with tears. I realized I was holding my throat with my right hand. Then she continued, "Every time I get to this part of the story, Nili, I really feel for these women. The entire neck rings procedure is preformed to ensure the fidelity of these women to their husbands. Sometimes their death will be brought about as a result of a rumor, gossip, or simply because the husband has a change of heart about being married to this woman.

"When a woman is found to be unfaithful, the village will hold a public trial led by the husband. In that ritual, the infidelity will be announced and her neck rings will be removed. The neck, which has lost its ability to support the head, will snap instantly, killing the woman."

Abigail noticed my look of disbelief. "That's why I brought you these pictures and the brass rings. I knew you wouldn't believe it. Look, in this last picture I'm sitting with them. This is how I can appreciate what I've seen."

Have I mentioned the fact that Abigail had been a registered nurse in her previous career? Well, no wonder she could articulate the physical condition of those necks trapped in the brass rings.

I picked up the last picture. It was surreal. The looks of those long-necked women and my friend Abigail sitting with them is a sight that stays in my memory.

I borrowed the pictures and the brass spiral rings, and brought them to the next group meeting. The evidence stunned the women who had shown a deep interest in learning about other civilizations. It turned out to be an unbelievable show-and-tell session. The pictures of healthy women whose necks had been tortured and manipulated caused anger and a shock I will never forget. The women reacted as strongly as they had to female circumcision— maybe even stronger. The implied cruel death sentence to women who appeared so alive brought on overpowering emotion.

The story left a strong impression on me too. In fact, during the winter break of the following year I took a similar trip into the jungle of northern Thailand. The trip was outlined for me in advance by Abigail. I was able to see the sights and the tribe she told me about.

Using the services of a local translator, I had the opportunity to interview one of the women of the tribe who was wearing brass rings. Ben, my husband, taped a video version of my conversation with the native woman. One of the questions I asked was why are you wearing the brass rings? The beautiful woman answered with no hesitation. "My parents told us that there are ferocious tigers out there, in the thick of the jungle. Those animals like to catch women by the throat. The rings protect us from the tigers."

During the following weeks, every group session contained a mention of some form of bodily mutilation and modification. Of course we were working on other issues too. I could see how there was an interest in the subject of the human body as a medium of expression, as some call it. In fact, to my surprise, they wanted more information.

Katherine was particularly fascinated. "Imagine the things whole populations choose to do to make themselves distinct from other nations," she said.

Tina could not pass this turn. "You mean like a national flag. No, wait, it's too close to their bodies; it's more like a team uniform. When you wear it, you feel a special belonging. I had that feeling once when playing softball. It felt really good to belong."

Beth agreed, "In our church we have color-coded T-shirts for each of the age-group activities. Guess what? The adults asked for the same color-coded tops for other nonsport activities that we have year round."

Rosie sighed and said, "But those things don't change your bodies permanently. They just make for easier recognition between groups."

"That is the point," I said. "Do we live in a civilization where the emperor or religion or the government can do this to us?" My voice was low and soft. Two women in the group, however, were intrigued.

Lisa jumped in and mentioned how male and female circumcision really bothered her. "The pain inflicted on them and the unnecessary suffering." I noticed her expression of empathy for other people's pain.

The second one to respond was Isabel, she answered slowly and thoughtfully stating that apparently we *do* live in such a culture. She added that peer pressure within one's culture seems to her to be as powerful as the law under some emperor or tribal chief.

As the women looked at her quizzically, my heart was pumping fast. A shot of adrenaline was introduced as my physiological reaction. I was sure I heard her say "powerful peer pressure." I was holding on to the arms of my seat, listening.

"I spent a summer in a camp once in the south of France," said Isabel. "It happened to be owned by the Jewish community. The majority of campers were Jewish, and the rest were Gentile kids whose parents were in the diplomatic corps. I'll never forget the fun the boys had picking on one of the youngsters. He was the cutest of the nine-year-olds whose parents—liberal Jews—did not believe in circumcision. The boys got on his case and picked on him the entire month. I felt so bad for him even though I didn't get it. Why were they picking on him? What is the deal? A few years later, I understood what it was about. Of course, it was about being different. He was not circumcised.

"The point I'm trying to make is not *only* about changing the human body. My concern is with the power the group or the culture assumes over an individual, even in the smallest group, in this case a miniature society of kids. They, the majority, I mean, empowered themselves with a mutual identity using that ritual. The ones who had not participated were made to feel as outcasts."

The following is from *Survival of the Prettiest* by Nancy Etcoff, Ph.D., about decorating the human body:

> Tattooing is believed to have originated in Nubia, in the fourth century B.C. The word derives from a Tahitian word, which means to strike. Tattoos have been made with boars' tusks, sea turtle shells, or fine needles, which are used to puncture the skin and inject dyes. In the nineteenth century Darwin found tattooed aborigines 'from the polar regions in the north to New Zealand in the south.'

Cicatrisation, or scarring of the body, is created by raising the skin into patterns with a knife or another instrument and is not uncommon in parts of the world where skin is dark and tattoos are hard to see. Piercing is practiced everywhere. Mummies have been found with elongated earlobes caused by the use of heavy earrings, and with two piercing in a single ear. People throughout human history have shoved shells, bones, feathers, and metallic objects through their ears and noses. They have pierced and bejeweled virtually every part of the face—the ears, noses, lips, eyebrows, and tongue—and all the erogenous zones of the body—navels, nipples, penises, and labias. Piercing in nerve-rich areas stimulate constant sensation, and viewers can't help but imagine these sensations as they look at the pierced skin. As such, the appeal is not so much visual in nature as tactile.

The following week, my friend Abigail called me to say she was leaving on another expedition, this time to Egypt. She wanted to show me another set of pictures she found in her collection. We met briefly and she told me about the adventure that she had on one of the islands of New Guinea beside the Septic River. She went there to explore the different cultures and found out about the "crocodile people." Again, she pulled out a set of pictures of young men and women whose bodies were covered with numerous scars on their backs, arms, faces, and legs. The scars had been made with a razor blade. The ritual is performed to show admiration and reverence to the crocodile. It is also marks the passage from childhood to adulthood.

As she passed me the pictures, she told me that not every boy and girl on that island must scar their body. The ones who do not go through with it, however, become second-class citizens and are not allowed into sacred places nor do they achieve high social status. Of those who become "crocodile people," many will die of severe infection since the process of scarring is not done under sterile conditions. The worse the scarring process, the more admired the final crocodile-like effect. Those young, beautiful, perfect human bodies with grotesque skin made my skin crawl.

When I shared with the group about this scary procedure, Angela had the strongest reaction. "I feel that on my inside! I'm as scarred as those 'crocodile-people.' They had to do it to be elevated and accepted to a higher status. I carry my scars on the inside. I'm not proud of them. Maybe those people are not proud either. Maybe they just accept social norms, afraid to insist on their right to be their own selves."

"Wait a minute," Jane said. "What exactly do you mean by acceptance to a higher status? You said it with so much pain."

"No offense, Ange," Tina said quickly. "You know how crazy I am about you. But you don't mean that your double breasts brought you a new elevation, literally." She winked at Angela who burst out laughing and gave us the comic relief we needed.

That, of course, was not what Angela meant, but her analogy was apt. Therapeutically, she made the leap of seeing her reality as one would look from the outside in. She understood the peer pressure among the "crocodile people" and identified with it. The scarring process that was desired in one culture became a sign of shame in another. Angela, who suffered from loss of self-respect, looked at herself as a weak person who let the "tribe" do it to her. Except the tribe in this case was our culture, embodied by her husband, Jim.

Lisa entered, as if on cue. The conversation had set off something in her. "I've wondered about this stuff," she said. "It touches me on several levels. Especially, I wonder about my new boobs and how they can make me so happy. But then I see Angela and how unhappy she is with hers."

Angela responded, "Lisa, changing your body demanded a lot of energy from you: excitement, anticipation, and finally the reward. This is not just your breasts and how they actually look, this is about your feelings about them."

Lisa answered, "I sometimes feel I was accepted into the club of sexy, cool babes and Angela's a charter member."

Angela continued, "And I feel I was expelled from what was normal, natural, and harmonious, and was pushed, controlled, and finally deformed into what I've called my double breasts."

Tina asked Angela, "What is going on? You sound so sad, maybe angry too. What are you feeling?"

Angela reacted. "Well, as you see, we live in a modern era, but for me, nothing has changed. They, I mean men, still manipulate my body, change it, deform it. Why do I participate in it? I've actually contributed to and surrendered to this process."

"I was thinking those exact thoughts about you just now," Beth said softly. "I didn't want to say it. It's so brave of you to say that yourself. There are so many emotions from you today. You look like you were trapped into this predicament. You are finally expressing yourself and battling this dilemma. It makes me feel good about this hard work we're doing here."

Rosie looked uncomfortable as she said, "What is this complimenting session about? Angela, you just said you identify with this part of anthropology. Do you feel like a helpless eight-day-old infant or a little Chinese girl who has nothing to say about her fate?"

Angela smiled at Rosie and nodded. "You see, I'm not physically small at all. I'm not handicapped in any physical sense, except emotionally. I'm a grown up and a self-sufficient professional woman with a career. Yet, I've been so blind. I keep reflecting on that one session that we had here long ago. Remember the time we talked about feelings about our feelings?"

"What about it?" Rosie did indeed remember it well.

Angela continued in an even softer tone. "How I wish I had told you then about all these feelings I have. I couldn't. I felt paralyzed. I felt trapped in my big breasts. I felt ashamed about my relationship at home, and I felt furious about having those feelings. This lesson in anthropology made me feel angry for these innocent people. But I could identify with them and see the helplessness in myself as well. How stupid could I have been?" Her face was energized. She did not cry. In fact, I detected a sort of smile on her face.

Grace noticed it too. "You don't look angry now. What's going on inside that head of yours?"

Angela smiled broadly. "The pain was always there. Now it feels as though I have some understanding by identifying with the 'crocodile people' in the story. My anger surfaced for a minute and I finally understand it. Actually, I'm enjoying the understanding part. Anger is still there, of course, and the shame of what I let my husband talk me into is there as well."

Pat looked at Angela and added, "It's an unconscious thing, I want to say, like brainwashing. Unlike the Chinese girls, there was no brainwashing necessary. They were so controlled. We are heavily influenced by fashion industries or something, and we are in it altogether."

Tina reminded Angela about the issue of feeling trapped. "If you've been trapped by those boobs," she said, "could it be a feeling of being overpowered by someone and just taking it out on your breasts?"

She had no chance to answer as Lisa jumped in. "Wait, you have helped me here a lot. I guess I've been booby-trapped by not having any breasts, the shame I felt about my body, the doubts about my femininity and all that. Am I making sense?"

Isabel, who was smiling, rescued her. "I hope you'll feel good about yourself regardless of the size of your breasts, Lisa. I think that our entire culture is severely booby-trapped. Look at us, the list is growing. Rosie who wants to be like Lisa, Tina with the American dream, Angela's husband, Beth's best friend Nina, Amy's breast-feeding fears and more. We are all trapped into thinking that there's an answer to our daily unhappiness, and it must be the size of our breasts. Relax, everybody. Better yet, get a life!"

n the literature on addiction, there are explanations for entire societies being addicted. The concept of being booby-trapped is a measuring stick to show the degree to which a person is addicted to an arbitrary societal norm—in this case, the look and size of women's breasts.

The women in the group reflect the majority of women in our culture who do not have a positive attitude about their breasts. The majority of women, however, develop positive attitudes about their skin, hair, nails, and even their hearts.

Many group discussions centered on our expectations about and disappointments in the "look" of our breasts and many women—both in the group and in society at large—are surprised to realize that how our breasts look is not as important as how they feel emotionally to us.

At the beginning of the group process, Lisa, Rosie, and Tina indicated they had never liked their breasts. It was Lisa who suggested that her new breasts, which she truly loves, have added a constant flow of erotic energy to her sex life. Tina compares Lisa's boob-job to the effect that Viagra has on men who take it.

Grace has never thought of respecting or liking her breasts. Her respect is reserved, however, for breast-feeding.

Pat hates, even fears, her breasts.

Katherine appreciates healthy breasts but has not "befriended" them until now.

Beth is the only one who has had a wonderful loving attitude all along. She has not yet singled out her breasts as objects of affection, and her relationship with her body inspires us all.

Chapter Nine

Don't Hold Your BREAST

Two Weeks Later

*The fight to restore the breast's nurturant sig-
nificance would be taken up at regular intervals during the centuries to come by individuals and groups opposed to the absolute reign of
the sexualized breast.*

> —from *A History of the Breast,*
>   by Marilyn Yalom

*...breasts are located in the fourth emotional
center, which is associated with the ability to
express joy, love, grief, and forgiveness, as well as
anger and hostility. If these emotions are blocked,
then the health of all the organs in the fourth
emotional center, which include the lungs and
heart as well as the breasts, may suffer.*

> —from *The Wisdom of Menopause,*
>   by Christiane Northrup, M.D.

WEEK AFTER WEEK, THE GROUP SESSIONS GREW MORE MEANINGFUL to the participants. Katherine, in particular, began to show us more of herself. While she had always been engaged in the therapeutic process, she acted more as a sympathetic listener and well-informed doctor. Now she was beginning to show us that she was open to exploring life beyond her job.

Most telling, she had hinted of a new man in her life but refused to elaborate when pushed, simply saying, "Let's wait and see."

I was confident she would eventually tell us more and so moved the rest to other topics. For Katherine, this was as much a part of a grieving process as anything. She, too, had lost some-one—her husband of five years, Richard. He had been a dedicated doctor—a burn specialist, whose young life, at age thirty-nine, was tragically cut short when the truck he was traveling in plunged over a mountainside. He was on his way to volunteer in a small Mexican village that had suffered the devastation of an earthquake. Since Richard's death, Katherine had been married to her job. This new man in her life was a big step for her.

The other news that startled many of the women came from Tina. She was seriously considering getting breast implants. "Just baby ones," she said. "I want a taste, a small one, of my American dream."

Beth, of course, did not approve, but many of the others were encouraging. This feeling of being emotionally supported—no matter what the issue or concern was—had provided remarkable emotional experiences to most of the women. And that quality was very much needed when Isabel signaled she had something to say.

Isabel informed us that she had to have some of her medical tests redone, but she did not have a real explanation why and con-fessed she had not been told herself. Katherine, of course, and a few others would not leave her alone until she communicated to us clearly regarding the nature of the tests. Having a medical degree and being in the public service, Katherine had developed an attitude of pragmatism that revealed her bedside manner: direct, assertive, managerial, and yet polite. As soon as she understood the nature of tests and Isabel answered some of questions, she made her own assessments. Katherine relaxed and became warm, personable, and empathetic. We watched Katherine do this with a few other women and learned to appreciate her complex personality, the physician and the woman intertwined. She was a great asset to us.

"I felt something in my breast weeks ago," Isabel began. "I waited to see if it had to do with my period or PMS, you know. Finally, my physician sent me for a mammogram. It's not clear yet to him what it is. I only know that I have noticed this lump in my breast for a few weeks. A second mammogram was ordered. The last thing I heard was that if it were malignant, it would have been stone hard. Mine is not hard, and the doctor said he is 90 percent sure it is not malignant."

Isabel kept her eyes only on Katherine as she related this to us. She looked tired and there were dark circles under her eyes. When she stopped talking, no one said a word. Finally, she added that during the week she would undergo more tests. Three women immediately offered to go with her. She thanked them and said she would call if necessary.

"Will Peter be able to be there with you if there is surgery?" Beth asked. We all knew that things had been rough between them.

"Well," Isabel said, "I really need him to go with me. I plan on asking him tonight. I have a feeling, however, he won't be able to." She was always honest about her own feelings. I had learned to listen to her and trust her reporting. She usually refrained from projecting onto others and did not hide vulnerable emotions. Again, she was reflecting on her true need for Peter to be there and on her inner knowledge that he was not there for her. We were astounded by the way she had accepted his new attitude. Isabel was scared and worried. Now she told us that Peter was nowhere to be found emotionally.

Rosie spoke up. "I always wondered what it would be like to be married to a handsome, successful professional man like Peter. I am envious, I guess. But why do you have to ask him to go with you? Wouldn't he volunteer and say I'll go with you, Isabel?"

Beth came to Isabel's defense. "We should let it be. Take it easy now, Rosie. Peter is not important now. Isabel said she would talk to him tonight. Also I think your curiosity about her marriage is a bit inappropriate."

There was a moment of uncomfortable silence.

The Eskimos have several words to describe the phenomenon of snow. In the same way, I've always believed therapists should have as many words to express the phenomenon of silence.

We all knew that something is wrong with this picture. And Rosie's timing was off. On second thought, Rosie's timing for Rosie was not off; she had started dating and the world of men was still a mystery to her. But as far as Isabel's needs were concerned, it was unacceptable to ask her about the relationship unless she brought it up.

The air felt thick and heavy. No one had said the word cancer yet. There had not been a diagnosis by a specialist, but already there was that feeling in the air—of a dread, and a heightened awareness.

The next week's session could not come soon enough. Each of the members of our group arrived earlier than usual, including me. Outwardly, we were calm. The ritual of the Daily Temperature Reading was a welcome tool that gave us the structure we needed. Isabel shared first—her appreciation for the show of support, new information about a specialist she was referred to, and her hopes to get over this hurdle in life. Isabel spoke as generally as she could, and still the word cancer was not mentioned. She told us about being retested and how, for the last forty-eight hours, she had been pacing, walking, and thinking.

"Thinking about what?" Jane's voice pierced Isabel's distant look.

She looked at us, focusing, it seemed, for the first time, and then said tremulously to Jane, "It's positive. They found a malignancy."

"Oh, no."

"My God, please, no."

"How can that be…"

No one paid attention to who had spoken, for it was as if everyone had spoken. I felt a lump of fear in my throat.

Isabel placed her right hand on her left breast, cupping her palm as if she were shielding the breast. She took a deep breath, then stretched out her right palm and stood up in front of her chair. For a second, she seemed like someone who was taking an oath. Her eyes were closed and her voice shook. "I need to say it so I can hear it myself and have you witness me saying it, and so I will know I said it." She took another deep breath. "My left breast has a malignant lump in it." She paused. "I have breast cancer." Then, like a litany, "I have cancer. Cancer. It was retested and confirmed. I have breast cancer. I can die."

She sat down very slowly, her eyes were closed. She raised her head and opened them. The room was spinning, at least for me. No one talked or moved or breathed. I wanted to scream. Instead, I closed my eyes for a brief moment, took a deep breath, and contained the impulse.

When I opened my eyes, nothing in the room had changed. I could not think quickly enough of an appropriate response to the moment, a response that would be professional. I heard myself saying, "Isabel, we are sorry, so sorry. What do you need from us now?"

My words, professional though they might have been, felt meaningless and weak. I was trying to stay with what Isabel needed now. Too often, a group would guess a person's needs and project their own emotions onto others. One group member would want "her" to cry helplessly. Another one might want "her" to get hysterical and lose control. While others might give medical advice. None was necessary; Isabel knew what she needed. She needed to hear the horrendous news from her own mouth. She had been courageous to stand up and state the unforgiving reality. I had to repeat my question, and finally she heard me.

After thinking for a moment, she answered, "I need you. I need to come here and say to you that I am afraid to die. I have been thinking for two days now how my world has shrunk down to my wish to survive. I am afraid to die. I don't want to die." She paused. "I have no idea where to start. My life is out of control. I'll be operated on the day after tomorrow. I don't believe I said that. The day after tomorrow is soon, but I have no idea what to do in the meantime."

She was crying. As I looked around the room, I realized, with no surprise, that everyone else was sobbing. The women sat in small groups of two or three, holding onto each other tightly. My face felt hot. I realized that I too was crying.

On the floor in the back of my office there is a pile of king-size pillows that I use sometimes for "anger work." We put them in the middle of the floor and created a safe place. Isabel was willing to cuddle into them, but she asked one member to sit with her.

Beth moved into the middle and Isabel, still crying, said to Beth, "I'm afraid; I'm scared to die." She repeated it many times over. The rest of the group sat beside her quietly. Isabel looked like she was slowly melting into the cushions, an adult shrinking back into the fetal position.

"I am scared," she said again. "I don't want to die. I have been so alone. Why is this happening to me? What have I done wrong?" She was sobbing now in Beth's arms. Her own tears flowed freely. Isabel's weeping sounded primitive, like a small baby gasping for air. It was the sound of despair and terror. A few hands caressed her shoulders and arms; some stroked her head and hair. Everyone comforted her or was comforted. I had placed myself near Beth, supporting her while she was supporting Isabel.

About twenty minutes later, when Isabel's sobbing sounded more under control, the women helped her move from the fetal position to a spot where she was leaning on her back. Isabel agreed to trust us holding her and relaxed into the circle of arms. For a moment we were quiet. Still crying softly, she had almost totally surrendered her body weight to our outstretched arms, all connected to warm, loving hearts.

Isabel opened her eyes and looked at us. Slowly she made eye contact with each of us. She saw that we were crying too. She looked at the flush faces, the tears, the running makeup, and the sweaty foreheads. Then her look fell to our supporting arms and, without a word, she reached out and caressed each one. No words were necessary. Her soft touch was comforting us as if to say everything is going to be all right.

While we were searching for ways to give her more support and strength, the most amazing thing happened. Isabel, who had grown quiet, said softly, "Would you rock me a little?"

By now she had totally surrendered her weight to our arms. We began to rock her gently back and forth, and the sensation gave us all pleasure. The amount of nurturing that poured out toward Isabel could not have been mistaken, and she took it all in. After about three minutes when she looked completely relaxed, I asked if she had a favorite lullaby. She told us. For the next ten minutes, we held her, supporting, singing, and weeping. Isabel was floating literally and figuratively. As for the rest of us, we were definitely being lifted high spiritually.

This emotional bonding lasted a long time. I realized that the formal session time had passed long ago. I asked the group to join me in a breathing and relaxing exercise. Once they were all mentally present, it was time to conclude the session. Isabel seemed to be back in control of her emotions. She was going from one person to another, receiving hugs and personal comfort.

When the group was seated back in their chairs, Isabel whispered, "That energy was so intense. Maybe I'm done crying. But how do I leave here today?"

What do you say to someone who is afraid to die? I was inspired by the expression of her fears. There was no masking or defending of emotions. Could I let the group go home so raw, without processing their feelings? I had asked for a silent moment and let them dry their tears. I gathered my energy and said a few more words—about Isabel's spirit, her appropriate need to be afraid, and our hope that she would be strong.

"Is there anything I should do just before my operation?" she asked. "I mean, is it possible that I am emotionally not ready for all this?"

"None of us would be completely ready in this case," Katherine said, sounding weak.

"Yes," I said, "there is some ritual I would like you to consider. It's time now to appreciate your breasts, to thank them for all the years of health and pleasures and sensuality. This may be a meditation or writing in your journal or a declaration. This is also the right time to say good-bye to your breasts as you have known them."

The group was crying again. I think that each one of us had unfinished grief, both for their own issues and for Isabel's. I said, "Let us pray now for Isabel's health, for the success of the operation, and the wisdom of the surgeons in charge."

We then left with a heavy heart. And Isabel was alone again.

Each one of us had an emotionally draining week. Not by comparison to Isabel's, of course. She had the shock of finding a lump, testing, guessing, theorizing, hearing the diagnosis, denying, and then confronting the facts.

Breast cancer has been a major problem in our generation. According to the American Cancer Society the rate of breast cancer is growing: 200,000 women will be affected by it this year. The women in this group had known that statistic since we had started to learn about breasts. That knowledge, however, did make the disease more frightening and their emotions more vulnerable.

At our next session, Pat brought in a book by Joyce Wadler called *My Breast*. It was a small book, yet filled with a wonderful emotional openness.

> I have spent a lifetime sorting things out with my friends. But now, I feel I am under attack, and when the Scud missiles are raining on your head, you don't have time to get on the phone with your girlfriends and say you are terribly depressed.

Pat read from this book in the next session too. She flipped through the pages she had painfully prepared to read. When she found the next quotation, she looked at us first and then looked down at the text. I never understood this, but now I do. Pat read:

> You don't tell the people you love, because you want to protect them. But in doing that, you cut yourself off. I talk to Nick about it. He says mothers are stronger than you think, and anyway, I owe my family the full story. The day after the biopsy, I call her.

Pat choked up on each line. The tiny book looked like a scary little package in her hands. Isabel's situation had provoked her and made her relive her personal trauma about her mother's death. Pat looked worried, anxious, and sleep-deprived. We asked her for her feelings and input.

The entire group had been going through an emotionally grinding time. Each woman identified on many levels with the fears and dreadful anticipation that Isabel was encountering. They all had spoken about breast cancer, and the awareness of that fear for some time now. The level of information and knowledge varied among them. Katherine and Pat were highly educated about the diagnosis, treatment options, and statistics on the disease. Some of the women had encountered major loss and grief. All knew relatives and friends who were well informed. A quick survey among us had revealed the astonishing fact that each one of us, without exception, had personally known a woman who had breast cancer.

This day we were ten women in the room. Isabel's absence was strongly felt. Each of us said out loud the name of a breast cancer victim dearest to her, a spontaneous act that was short and extremely powerful. Beth suggested standing up as we mentioned the individual's name. The group lovingly agreed and made it into a ritual. This was a therapeutic as well as a spiritual moment. Pat mentioned Susan, her mother.

My own family lost my second cousin, Lilly, to the disease. She was only thirty-two years old.

Pat pointed out another paragraph, at the end of the book, where there is a chapter by Dr. Susan Love. Considering the fact that it was written in 1992, the statistics are likely different today.

> Breast cancer is an epidemic. One in nine women will develop breast cancer in her lifetime, and breast cancer is one of the diseases women fear most. Joyce Wandler's story depicts the turmoil women go through when they get this diagnosis; the thirst for information to guide them through the maze of treatment options; the fear they experience facing a potentially life-threatening disease.

Lisa shared about her emotional week. Her account reflected a lesson in Lisa's adult development. "Let me try to tell you how it feels from where I come from. Isabel is not here today, and God only knows what she is going through. Her tragedy has triggered something in me. I'm not sure of the meaning of it all. Isabel supported me in the past, and I've felt a strong connection with her. In a nutshell, I feel guilty and somewhat ashamed for the joy and celebration I've had about my boob job. It's been very important to me to go through that transition.

"This past week's events gave me another perspective on the importance of my breasts though. I am becoming aware of the—what?—frailty of the human body. My breasts, which I used to consider a sexual symbol, are more meaningful for me. They were like a toy, a pet, an object of affection. I still would have gotten the implants. But I never considered the full picture before. I've been thinking about it though, and I couldn't find any peace of mind. Why is it that everything revolves around our breasts? Am I the only one who feels this way?"

"You've got something there," Katherine said. "I was thinking about it last night. Not the sexual part but the growing hazard of simply being a female. We have to go through our life preventing breast cancer."

Rosie broke in and told us how disturbed she was with the subject of death. "First, I thought of Isabel for three days. Then I cried for a long time. I said to myself I'm scared of life anyway, so now here's a real reason to stay scared. After a week of doing nothing but worrying about Isabel, I realized that I am scared about myself. I am always afraid. What a week it has been! Months ago, I shared with you about my fear of life." She paused, and then looked at each of us and said, not without some dread in her voice, "Now I am afraid to die."

Tina sighed and said how much she wished she could do something for Isabel. Then she looked at Katherine. "Breasts and death. What a pair! I have been pairing those together since my childhood. Ever since I learned about those Japanese prostitutes who died for so-called better breasts. Some of them died in misery. Breasts are dangerous stuff, implants or no implants. I am scared for Isabel. I am scared for all of us." After this outburst, she stared at the floor.

Jane pulled out a printed page from her brown leather brief-case. She smoothed it out with both hands and said she wanted to read to us a passage from a wonderful book called *Bosom Buddies,* by Rosie O'Donnell and Dr. Deborah Axelrod.

Who gets breast cancer?

There are many myths about who gets breast cancer, and what causes it. The fact is, anyone can get breast cancer. It's far more common in women, but men can get it, too. Young people get breast cancer; old people get it, too. Rich people get it, and so do the poor. People of all races and ethnicities get breast cancer. Large-breasted women get it; and small-breasted women get it. And despite the many myths about what raises risk, the majority of women have no identifiable risk factors and 90 percent have no significant family history of the disease.

Another prevalent myth about breast cancer is that women who live basically healthy lives—who exercise, eat a healthy diet, don't smoke, and don't drink—don't get it. Unfortunately, while clean living reduces the risk of many cancers and other major diseases, and certainly makes you feel better, it offers no guaranteed protection against breast cancer. No one is immune to this disease.

Jane put the paper down and looked at me. Her face was pale as she said, "I'm *afraid* of that thing, you know."

The rest of the women shared similar feelings of helplessness and fear.

We had no news about Isabel's condition, but tomorrow we would. The group made no attempt to conceal their real feelings of despair and gloom. They had been nearly traumatized by the recent events. They were sad and quiet.

Minutes went by and no one said a word. Suddenly, a noise disturbed the stillness of the room. I was not sure at first what it was, but then I saw the little book Pat had been holding. It flew across the floor and landed in the middle of the room.

The contrast between our quiet thoughts and the book's violent punctuation startled us. I did not respond right away. Pat held her face in her hands. When she looked at us, we saw that her face was flush, red and angry, and streaked with tears.

"I can't take this any more," she cried. "I hate Isabel, I hate this life, and I don't have the energy to go on. This is not going to end now. Every time you look away, there will be another one dead. Breasts are everywhere, but they only cause pain and death. I hate breasts! They'll betray you. They'll kill you." She fell silent and Jane touched her shoulder and called her by name. Pat burst into tears, half-talking, half-weeping. The only comprehensible words I could recognize sounded like "Don't go," "Why," "I am not ready." It seemed she was pleading, bargaining with someone.

Pat was agitated and highly emotional. Her mood swings were mild in comparison to this reaction. This was the first time Pat experienced an emotional outburst of this magnitude. She rocked back and forth in her chair, her arms wrapped around herself. She looked weak and fragile, almost unable to talk. The transformation had been fast. An hour ago, she had been sad but composed as she read to us. What had triggered the transformation? She would not answer me. She did not know.

The group was supportive and receptive. No one gave advice or told her how she should feel. They were more vulnerable than ever, identifying with Isabel, and feeling afraid for themselves. Isabel's tragedy and our exposure to the turmoil were creating an opportunity for all of us to experience and express unconscious feelings. Our little group had developed an in-house sort of lingo. One of the phrases we used affectionately among ourselves was "Taking a free ride on something." Such were our fears regarding breasts that we were "taking a free ride" on these emotional circumstances, projecting, and relating them to our own situations.

Apparently, Pat was embarking on the beginning of a new journey. Her emotions that surfaced—the sadness, the anger, and the rage—confused her. Provoked by the chain of events, she had been thrown into this free ride. Pat was reexperiencing the trauma of the years before the death of her mother: the years of testing, diagnosis, choices for treatments, doubts, examination of side effects, and finally the end. As she read from the book, the absence of Isabel, the faces of the group members—all stimulated her consciousness.

And the emotional floodgates opened. Years of unspoken anger broke through her emotional dam. Pat's feelings and thoughts, I explained to the others, passed through her faster than she could process them—which we all sometimes experience—and they spilled out. Some of the emotions were not familiar to her. At the same time, some emotions were familiar but unacceptable to her.

Tina reacted first. "Wait, what do you mean by 'unacceptable to her'? Isn't remembering all that history painful enough?"

"Let's ask Pat," I suggested. She was back in our focus.

Tina turned to Pat. "I followed most of your feelings and reactions, but it must have been hell for you. What is it with unacceptable feelings? Is it an attack of feeling about the feelings thing? How can anything be unacceptable to you after all these years of anguish?"

"I have been struggling with this for a long time," said Pat. "First in dreams, during the night, I would be awakened by this horror, the sight of people being eaten alive by aliens. I have never resolved those dreams. I used to wake up shaken. I couldn't get back to sleep. Walking around tired for days caused me to have the most bizarre thoughts. I had moments when I did not want to take care of my mother who was getting sicker. I did not want to participate in this dying process. I had so much anger inside and nowhere to go with it. She died and I am afraid I died with her. Emotionally, I mean."

Beth moved uncomfortably in her seat. "Do you still have those nightmares?"

"Yes, they have come back since Isabel got sick. I have been so angry with Isabel too. This has been too much for me. I am ashamed to share this, but I am mostly angry with Isabel, just like I was with my mom."

Grace said softly, "We have not asked you yet what you are angry about. We are so sad about this development and maybe we want to protect you from these intense feelings. Please tell us about this unacceptable anger you are carrying."

Pat looked even more helpless than before. She said she did not understand that the anger was pathological grief, as her grief therapist had told her. She simply could not find peace of mind, could not let go of her mom.

"What is it about the anger that is coming back to you?" Grace asked.

Pat started to say she didn't know but stopped and started again. "I've had no chance to share everything I needed to say. I said all the please-forgive-me stuff and many I-love-yous. You know what I mean. I've said it all. And I still cannot go on with my life. What am I to do? Should I get breast cancer, too? And die?"

There was a dead silence; one of those moments when you wish a person's words would just go away. But they never do.

I felt that if Pat were made angry enough, maybe she would let some of the poison out. "What is it about the relationship that was missing," I asked, "before all the good-byes and the final I love-yous?" I looked directly at her and she returned my gaze.

"With my mom?" she said.

She's stalling, I thought, but I let her set the pace.

"Pat," I said, "you mentioned a few minutes ago that maybe you should get breast cancer too. What was that about? Must you be just like Mom?" I was shooting in the dark, but the dynamic between a mother and daughter was a predicament I had treated before. I was not wrong.

"I cannot help it," Pat said. "I liked everything she liked. I would have loved to be like her in so many ways."

"And how different were you and your mom?" I insisted.

"In so many things. My mom was so perfect and I am such a loser. She was smart and sexy and interesting and energetic and…"

I stopped her. "I'm much more interested in what you are and not in the eulogy to your mom."

Pat was startled. "I don't know what to say about myself. I could never climb to her level and now that she is dead, I really have no chance." Now we were getting somewhere.

"A chance for what?" I asked, throwing the ball back to her so fast she gasped.

Pat caught her breath, and then shot back, "I wanted the chance to show her that I can be a better mother!"

"What?" Beth said.

Grace broke in, "You mean you could have been better in doing motherhood than you had done schooling or typing or something?"

"No," Pat said. "I mean I think I wanted to show her that I could be a better mother than she ever was."

The group refused to "get it." It was a tough concept. It had been many months that we had been admiring this goddess-like woman, Susan. Now in one fell swoop, we were told the idol had feet of clay.

Lisa began muttering, "I don't get it. I don't get it."

Rosie was practically crying.

Tina said, "Hello, we are still talking about Susan, right?"

Beth gave it her best. "Your mom, according to you, was not an adequate mother for you? We used to think she was the best of the best, as you used to say. Wasn't she?" Beth tried to control her own voice.

Pat smiled, although nothing appeared amusing. She was now willing to share the burden she had been carrying alone for years. She retold the story we had already heard about her mother, but with a different slant.

Pat told us that she had not lied about her mother. She herself had not admitted the truth until recently. It had been unraveling slowly since Isabel's diagnosis, and now she could not contain the anger Isabel's situation had provoked in her.

The puzzle began to come together. The anger was her clue; our relentless questioning and encouragements brought the conflict to the surface. The first clear piece of her puzzle was her mother refusing to breast-feed her when she was born. There would be more to come.

"Susan was self-conscious about the appearance of her breasts," she said. "She simply did not want them to sag. She told her best friends that and they joked about it among themselves."

"Here we go again," said Lisa with a dramatic sigh. "Another breast story. It's been a long time since we've mentioned them."

Pat, who was exhausted by now, wanted to return to the story and get it over with. "No, Lisa," she said, "don't hold your breasts. That is not the main story." We all burst out laughing and Pat looked around wonderingly. Then she got it. "I don't believe I said that," she let out, laughing.

Tina seized the moment. "Honey, look again. Our Lisa does not need to hold her breasts. They are just fine, thank you."

The rest of the session flowed with questions and answers. Pat shared unhesitatingly about the myth and reality of Susan, about how a superwoman did not have time to nurture her daughter. Then she also shared some childhood fantasies about her mother having an accidental death, secretly wishing she could get a better mom!

Until now Pat had forgotten those childhood wishes. Instead, she had protected herself by adoring, admiring, and idealizing Susan, so she made sure every person that got close to her would admire Susan too. Her secret was safe. But then Susan got sick and died. Pat was left alone with her secret wishes struggling to surface from her tortured unconscious. The circle was completed.

Through her primitive and childlike memories, she wanted to punish her mother. In her dreams she saw aliens, but the flesh-eating killers were not about the cancer. It only sounded like that. The dreams were about Pat's alien anger, wanting Susan's death. That is how the unconscious works, camouflaging the meaning so one is able to sleep. No one would have ever guessed that such a drama would have emerged, that the memory of a little girl wishing to punish her mom for lacking mothering skills disappeared, buried under an edited admiration. Isabel's struggles with her life removed the mask from those memories. Through it, Pat gave herself permission to put those feelings to rest.

As we were leaving the room, Rosie said, "Psychology. It's so complicated and mysterious, isn't it?"

"Nah," Grace answered and winked. "It's all in your head."

Chapter Ten

Beauty, and the Beast, and the BREASTS

One Month Later

> *Breast cancer remains by far the most common cancer among women worldwide, and the leading cause of death in American women aged forty to fifty-nine.*
>
> > —from *Bosom Buddies,* by Rosie O'Donnell and Deborah Axelrod, M.D.

> *What we can do—whether we're looking back on a cancer experience, helping someone else through a cancer experience, or living through the horror right this minute—is tell our story. Stories help. Stories heal. Your story might be the very thing that saves someone's life or helps them get through the night. It might be the only thing that brings you a measure of peace.*
>
> > —from *The Victoria's Secret Catalog Never Stops Coming,* by Jennie Nash

SHE MADE IT. ISABEL I MEAN. IN HER ABSENCE WE ALL FELT THAT we had spent a lifetime together. Values to live by were reevaluated. Life and death were reexamined. Fear of breast cancer and fear for life intensified the quality of our communication and the commitment to be there for each other like a sisterhood. Since I had identified myself with all those feelings, I could have easily recognized two strong emotions among the group members: genuine empathy with Isabel's struggle and a raw fear for our own lives.

The day had arrived and she came back. Our Isabel. Pale, slender, and somewhat older. It had been four weeks since she had participated in a group meeting. It felt like a whole year. Again, it was Lisa who brought up the subject of Isabel's marriage relationship. Beth urged her to wait until next time. We agreed to wait since we really needed a reunion session with Isabel. Indeed, Isabel wanted simply to be grateful for her life and to appreciate our involvement and caring. She really was a gentle soul and a gracious woman, and her expressions of appreciation were genuine.

I must admit, we were a terrific group of sisters to Isabel. She told us that our capabilities for nurturing and caring were the envy of all of her friends and relatives.

Isabel felt weak and interested in healing her body and soul. She joined a group that specialized in healing the aftermath of breast cancer. Her daily life revolved around making herself healthy again. She had renewed energy about everything, and she could not wait to report about her progress.

"I've changed my entire way of eating," she said on her first day back. "There are so many fine things about life. I'm definitely learning a lot at my cancer survivors group. For example, besides nutrition, I started a yoga class." She looked at Beth. "Well, Beth, just like you always said, yoga is good for the body and soul. What makes it easy during the day is the meditation. And that brings me to you, Grace. Thanks again for reminding me about the power of meditation. And there is also my journaling."

"Remember how we were asked to write in our journal? Dr. Nili had to teach us the value of it, but I don't think I put my heart into it. Well, I was watching *Oprah* on television a few times a week, especially the last two weeks. I'm impressed. I saw the power of journaling on her show. There's a lot to learn about keeping a gratitude journal, and I want to start one again. Actually, I write a few lines every day and now I am committed to it."

She could not stop talking about how she was experiencing life. We learned about the special oils she was using, the special tea she drank, and the "no-no's" we should give up for the sake of our own health. We listened with love, nodding, smiling, agreeing, and taking her in. She was like our child who had been lost and now was fortunately found.

Her prognosis was excellent. We were reassured by both her physician and our in-house doctor Katherine that Isabel would be fully recovered soon. Her life was actually saved by early detection of breast cancer. During her recovery period, the group shared their personal fears of the incomprehensible calamity of breast cancer. Rosie first referred to it as a black hole, and we eagerly adopted the term as a resonant analogy. Witnessing Isabel's stages of recovery had brought the mystery of this disease back to us. Who will get it next? Why? When? What are the chances of survival? The questions, unvoiced, nevertheless were present in our minds. We all knew this black hole was "out there" and every so often, an innocent person's life would be sucked into it.

Weeks after her last reconstructive surgery, Isabel expressed gratitude for being alive. Her responses to surviving cancer were a great inspiration to all of us. She read us a paragraph from her gratitude journal, concluding, "Life belongs to the living and I am living it up." She smiled and looked renewed. If surviving breast cancer was anything like getting married, Isabel was certainly still on her honeymoon. She tasted life again. "Smelling the roses is not a cliché to me," she wrote. "I actually take time to do that now."

She also became fascinated with science and the invention of breast implants, which the group had discussed before. Grace made an observation: "Who would have known we would all look at those plastic bags, filled with saline water, as a wonderful alternative after breast cancer, the beast. I remember well Lisa's show-and-tell, Amy's desires, Rosie's envy, Tina's American dream, and Angela's double breasts. It's amazing to me how it all seems so far away, small in significance. Almost as if it were another lifetime."

Isabel was open to all alternatives. At one point, she had been introduced to Terry, a breast cancer survivor who argued against reconstructive surgery. Terry told her that it would take several surgeries and that she, Terry, had decided to heal her scar and go on with her life. Isabel was impressed with Terry who was her same age. We also heard through Isabel that Terry's husband had encouraged her not to reconstruct her missing breast. He told her that he had fallen in love with her, not with her breasts. The group applauded him, especially Beth, Grace, and Jane. Lisa, on the other hand, could not believe a man would say—let alone think—such a thing. But Isabel had studied the alternatives, consulted her physician, and made her decision in favor of having breast implants.

Our group process had been intensified by the reality of Isabel's life, so the main subject we discussed now was breast cancer. We read a great deal. We were all interested to know more about the nature of this beast, sharing numerous books, articles, Web sites, and other resources.

Tina read this interesting paragraph from *Bosom Buddies:*

There is some well-known data about Japanese women moving from Japan to the United States. It appears that women have relatively low rates of breast cancer in Japan, and their rates climb significantly when they reach the United States. The increase in risk is especially pronounced among first-, second-, and third-generation migrants. Why? Could it be the change in diet? A change in weight? A change in chemicals in the air? A change in pesticides in foods? Postponed childbearing? All of the above? There is a great deal of interest in what makes for changes in the risk of breast and other cancers with migration from place to place.

Someone else read from *Women's Bodies, Women's Wisdom:*

Breast cancer is the leading cause of cancer death among American women who are forty to fifty-five years of age.

Dealing with the medical aspects of breast cancer was not the goal of the group, but we had special feelings reading from this book. In fact, by the time Isabel was operated on, each of us owned a copy. We each were impressed with Christiane Northrup's thinking and writing. Many of the women shared this information with their friends and relatives, all of whom were greatly affected by it.

In my experience, inner reflective work to change emotional patterns associated with breast cancer, certain types of support groups, and dietary improvement are important parts of treatment, regardless of whether one has a lumpectomy or undergoes mastectomy, radiation or chemotherapy.

Later in the book, Dr. Northrup described her understanding that breast cancer results when most of our energy is tied up dealing with old hurts. In the case of Isabel, the time had come to examine the core relationship she was in. Or was she still in this relationship?

Our group became one of the major support systems in Isabel's recovery. We were a strong and committed family for her. She called us "my sisterhood." But even with all the support, her process of healing was slow. It was obvious to me she had become a "recovery expert," which was admirable. Part of her recovery, however, was not happening, in particular the emotional connection at home. I held back from initiating the subject to give her the space she needed. It would be painful, as I had known it to be so in the past. Dealing with her marriage would require all of her strength and our support.

Initially, we decided to shelve this subject until Isabel was stronger, but finally, when Lisa could not tolerate it any longer, she asked Isabel about Peter's whereabouts during surgery. Isabel tried to explain that he disliked doctors and hospitals. Those excuses, however, did not sit well with us.

We found out from Isabel that her Peter, who had always been emotionally distant, was displaying some highly unusual behaviors. He was now totally absent, both emotionally and physically. The fact that he had not accompanied Isabel when she went for her tests and diagnostic appointments was odd and difficult to understand. Isabel however, showed no signs of being willing to deal with him under her present circumstances. Her disappointment was squashed beneath the crisis. Simply put, her survival was more important than teaching priorities and manners to Peter. Isabel dismissed Peter's behavior as childish and seemed comfortable not talking about him.

We could not help noticing he was nowhere to be found the day of her surgery. Yet, we were there, taking turns at Isabel's bedside. Three of us even spent the night in the hospital with her. Peter had not shown up until four days later.

This upset us, as it had Isabel, and finally, after our prodding, she confessed that Peter had been buying prostitutes' sexual services, and frequenting an adults-only store. He spent large amounts of time and money. These were unaccounted for throughout the time of surgery and recovery. There had been, it turned out, a history of this behavior. At the time of Isabel's diagnosis and surgery, Peter's behavior had gotten worse, and his sexual addiction had become a major health concern for Isabel. She decided to pursue marriage therapy for both of them, and Peter had agreed to participate.

As Isabel became stronger, she grew more interested in Peter's disorder. His dynamics were clinically familiar: intense sexual activities. Those acts do not take into consideration what is morally wrong or hazardous to his or another person's health. Anything goes. And at any cost—literally at any cost—marriage, money, and one's own health. In our culture, mostly men, and to lesser extent women, are afflicted with sexual addiction. Their behavior masks a clinical depression that is treatable. Because they are not in touch with their depression, they create a secretive double life that masks their own emotions from themselves.

The group explored this disorder carefully. Beth had known a couple of cases. One man had to leave her congregation, since his conduct was not appropriate to the church members' code of ethics. I gave a short lecture about sexual addiction and the clinical aspects of the disorder.

Isabel had many questions that were left unanswered. One pertained to the recommended treatment of sexual addiction. I was familiar with two types of treatments. The best one is performed at residential addiction centers where the patient checks in for a month at a time for intensive psychotherapy. The second choice would allow a person to stay at home and attend daily twelve-step groups, in addition to psychotherapy.

Isabel's honeymoon was sadly over, and for her, she said the beast was not breast cancer, but the mental illness in her marriage. She decided to follow through with a legal separation. It was a difficult decision. She waited to hear from Peter regarding his recovery decision. He did not want to choose the residential treatment. He also did not agree to participate in any twelve-step programs nor did he continue the marriage counseling they had started.

It turned out that Peter had been mildly sexually addicted for several years. His confrontation with the possibility of Isabel's death from breast cancer helped the disorder to erupt. There was also the possibility he had been abusing alcohol or other substances, since sexual addiction often accompanies substance addictions.

Isabel had known about Peter's conduct for some time. Now, she was relieved that the other women knew about Peter too.

Angela was also involved in a process of rediscovering her own marriage path. She commented that both Peter and Isabel were cooperating within their disorder. "I don't mean that Isabel has a sexual disorder, but probably—like myself—you are at least an enabler of sorts."

Those in the group who had been in significant relationships immediately understood Angela's concept. We had all been there except Lisa, who of course demanded an explanation. Jane and Grace began to speak, but it was Beth who brought in a story from a book she was reading, *The Personality Disorders,* by James F. Masterson. The story she chose illustrated a relationship in which the unavailability of the lover was the attractive quality:

> Two couples are on a cruise together, and the man in one couple starts an affair with the woman in the other couple. At the end of the cruise, the man of the one couple has fallen in love with the woman and tells her he is about to divorce his wife. The woman in the other couple says that's fine for you, but if you ever get married again, look me up.

Isabel had grown emotionally since her diagnosis was announced. An irreversible process had begun, that which had brought on the fear of death had also opened her heart to see what she wanted in this life. Consequently, Isabel had to mourn her relationship and marriage. They were over. This was difficult to accept for some of the other women who had unresolved relationships.

This led to discussions on the predicament of individuals, couples, and families when their lives were invaded by breast cancer.

"What goes on in the minds of those husbands?" Tina asked after Jane had described a childhood friend of hers who survived cancer and whose husband left her.

I also shared two examples from my other therapy groups about husbands who had deserted their wives in the midst of their battle for survival. One of the men reconsidered and reconciled with his wife. Now they are working through the crisis. The second couple had a history similar to Isabel's, except the husband was not sexually addicted. He had, however, fallen in love with another woman he wanted to marry.

We were dealing with new information that Rosie could not digest. "I don't get it," she said, hardly able to remain in her seat. "I just don't get it. What do they want? What makes them run like that?"

Lisa tried to reaffirm her situation. "See, I told you all along. Boobs are very important. They can break up a marriage."

"Be quiet, little girl!" Beth exploded. "Looks like you still don't get it, after all this investment we're making in you. Can't you see the hurt? The breakup of families? The twisted minds of these men?"

"Beth, just relax. Let's do this differently," I said. "Can you remember a session in the past in which we mentioned other women who were victimized by breast cancer?" The tension in the room eased as I asserted my authority. "Recently, however, we realized that each one of us knows a woman who had breast cancer, survived it, and lost her husband in the process. Not lost him to death, mind you, but to his *fear* of death. What a mind-blowing idea." I waited a few moments while they caught my meaning.

Grace spoke first. "Are you saying that men who leave women who have survived or are struggling with breast cancer are *not* one-in-a-few-million cases? Rarities?"

"I've heard about this from a social worker in the hospital. It's no rarity I'm sorry to say." Katherine's voice was soft but clear.

There was a giggle in the room. We all stopped and looked around. Jane was smiling and asked if anyone could recall the movie *Moonstruck*. Most of us did. It was a favorite of mine.

"What about it?" Lisa asked, impatiently.

"Well," Jane said, still smiling. "I don't know what made me think about this part. Anyway, I remember Olympia Dukakis in the mother role. She rightfully suspects that her husband is cheating on her and she wants some answers. She asks a stranger why men do it, and she is amazed at his answer. They are afraid to die."

I recalled this scene in the movie and was grateful to Jane for the appropriate bridge she had created. I smiled at her. Beth got it, too.

"I remember the part," Angela said. "I liked that movie, too, but what is the message?" She looked at Lisa and they both agreed they wanted more expansion on the subject.

Tina jumped into the conversation. "I've been telling you for many months now. Boobs and death. Get it already: boobs and death. Men are scared of the death that might come with breast cancer. They run away." She paused. Everyone was listening. Jane nodded in agreement.

"Some men don't know what to do within the proximity of death, or a major loss, and they must escape," Jane said. She was enjoying her moment. "I have a few examples myself. My neighbor started an affair while his wife was having a mastectomy. I tell you, they run fast."

Rosie looked uncomfortable. "So what is it? A new social disease?" She was serious and worried.

"You see, Rosie," I said, looking straight at her, "with the prevalence of breast cancer among women today, we will see more abandonment of women. There is no public awareness of the need to educate people. Death and the threat of death are very scary and most of us—women and men—don't know how to deal with the emotions it raises."

Now Rosie looked even more agitated. "You're actually saying that we'll witness more women being left in the midst of this fight for their lives?"

"What I'm saying, Rosie, is that we have an epidemic of breast cancer. So many more women will become sick, I'm sorry to say. Their lives will be threatened. Some men cannot tolerate the strong emotions that develop during this time, and therefore they might want to defend against what they feel is a threat to them. You know about fight or flight, don't you?" She nodded.

Isabel found more energy to deal with the issue. "So is this the picture? He is scared and running like crazy?" She looked at me.

"Yes and no," I said, understanding her need. "Isabel, in your case, it is not as simple. Peter has what they call in the administration of medicine a 'preexisting condition.' Namely, for a few years now, he has had a mild case of sexual addiction. The death threat that your breast cancer represented pushed him over into a full-blown addiction. He ran away to hide when the threat for your life was over. He started to act out in a most dangerous way. It helped him deny his own feelings toward you and his own mortality. His refusal of treatment makes the future of the marriage impossible. Are you with me?" The group was silent.

Isabel said, "Yes, I know, I know. I guess you're saying that he is scared and crazy." She smirked and looked around at the others. Her expression made everyone smile.

"Make no mistakes," I said seriously. "I want to bring in another kind of illustration here. I have a friend who is also a colleague; we'll call him David. David married his wife who was a survivor of breast cancer. He had known of her condition when they met and fell in love. David's wife was cancer-free for a few wonderful months. Then the cancer reoccurred. He was there to nurture her and take care of her all the way until her death. They comforted each other, bless his heart. There are real men out there like David and I want you to know that." I stopped and realized that Isabel was crying. She was touched by my story and felt sad.

From the corner came Pat's voice, soft and vulnerable. "Was my reaction to my mom's breast cancer a flight or a fight?"

Such a good question, I thought. "What do you think, Pat?"

She was embarrassed and became quiet. "I didn't run away. I nursed her for a few years. I wonder why I even asked you."

Jane answered her. "You were really there for her."

Angela added, "I was always impressed with your ability to stick by her for so long."

Tina joined in. "What do you want from Pat? She knows she was terrific. So give her a break. She must have some more feelings here, otherwise she would not ask that." Tina was right on target, and the group let Tina continue what she had started. "I gather that a part of you was not there with your mom. So spit it out. We're here and we're not going anywhere."

Pat looked up with some relief. "Tina, you're right. I was not honest with Mom. I nursed her with all of my heart. But, you know, emotionally I think I had to hide. I had a double life. As you know, I didn't tell her about my disappointments about her performance as a mother. My expectations were never met. I feel that physically I did 'fight.' But emotionally I'd done the 'flight' thing. I realize now that my mom never knew me because I didn't want her to know me."

Angela spoke up. "What am I missing? What didn't you want your mom to know about you and why is it important now?"

Pat looked pale and uneasy as she said, "I didn't want her to know I am gay. She'll never know. She'll never know." She would not look up at our eyes.

Then Pat spoke again. "I'm sorry to lay it on you like that." She sounded embarrassed.

"I've been waiting for you to say that for several months," Angela said, disturbing the silence. "I'm so glad you did."

Rosie gave a loud sigh and said, "I didn't know about your being gay. Thanks for sharing, I guess. I mean, I don't know what to say."

Beth wanted to know if Pat had feelings about being gay or was she a practicing lesbian. Pat looked at her quizzically. Beth asked again, "Do you have experiences as a lesbian or are you thinking about relationships with women?"

Pat thought for a moment and said, "This is easier than I anticipated. I don't have any past intimate experiences with women and very few unsuccessful ones with guys." She had regained her composure now.

Lisa asked, "So how do you know about women? I mean, that you're gay?"

Grace said, "Take it easy on her, Lisa. She said she knows, didn't she?"

"All right," Pat said. "I guess I've had special feelings toward women for some time. I have stronger feelings for and sexual attractions to women since I told the truth about my mom a few months ago."

"You know," Tina said with a warm, caring tone in her voice, "you do make a lot of sense to me now that I see the whole picture. I hope you didn't suffer too much keeping all that in. I'm glad you shared and have come out."

I had not said a word for some time, which was a good sign for the psychological development of the group. They were proving they could deal with major emotional situations and be, for the most part, nonjudgmental.

The discussion went on to clarify what sexual attraction is, that is if one can be homosexual without the actual sexual experience with same sex partners. And we discussed whether Pat had any sexual fantasies about any members of the group.

Rosie, who was confused by the entire subject, raised this last question. "I sometimes do that; I may experience a fantasy without wishing it," she said. "They appear in my mind without me controlling it." Pat agreed, but would not name any particular person. And we let it be at that.

Chapter Eleven

BUSTED!

Three Weeks Later

I was always amazed at how much my friends' breasts had affected their perceptions of themselves as women. What other body part is that powerful?

—from *Breasts,* by Meema Spadola

Given our cultural inheritance about our breasts, it is little wonder that women's fear of breast cancer far overshadows our risk for those things that are more likely to kill us either directly or indirectly, such as heart disease or being battered by a husband or boyfriend.

—from *The Wisdom of Menopause,*
by Christiane Northrup, M.D.

WHILE OUR ATTENTION HAD BEEN DEVOTED TO THE BIGGER drama of breast cancer, we turned to some "dating" events taking place among the single women in the group. Apparently Lisa was still seeing Jeff. We did not know much about him, since Lisa's conversations were typically focused on his looks. We knew about his height, his dark hair, his smile, and his general good nature. We did not know, however, about Lisa, the person, in the context of this relationship.

Still, this had been the longest time we had witnessed Lisa being interested in just one man. When they first began to date, Lisa sounded entertained, as she usually was when she was attracted to a man. I did not notice that this particular experience of dating Jeff was more prolonged than the others and had matured into a steady relationship.

"He is so different from the usual guys I've met before," Lisa said. "I swear he is totally of another kind. He's so special to me. I've turned down two other guys who keep calling me and told them I am going out only with Jeff."

"What makes him so special?" Angela asked.

"Well, for one thing," Lisa said, "he's smart. He's an animator. I don't mean like Mickey Mouse, but those complicated, high-tech things like Steven Spielberg does. You know, *Star Wars*-like stuff. And he thinks them up, too, not just designs them. He's also funny, and I don't mean ha-ha funny but, you know, like..." she paused.

"Witty?" Tina said.

"Yeah!" Lisa said. "Like clever, which you all know I'm not."

"What else?" Jane asked.

"Well, he's nice. I don't mean just nice, but really kind. And..." she said, pausing, then she giggled. "And when I told him I'd had a boob job, he simply asked why."

We broke into laughter.

"He does sound special," Beth said laughingly.

The reactions were sweet and unanimously encouraging. "All right, Lisa!" "Congratulations!" "Good job, girlfriend!" "Now you're talking." "Good luck, Jeff!"

What was it about Lisa that caused adult women to react like a bunch of cheerleaders?

Isabel had been attending her cancer recovery group regularly. She had decided to file for divorce instead of staying legally separated. The recovery group had strongly recommended ending all nonnurturing relationships, especially the abusive ones. She felt stronger and the decision empowered her even more.

"Finally, I have full control over my life. I want to be the one who says what goes on in my life and when."

She felt even better after the actual filing. The grief over the marriage was nearly over. Isabel would not be ready for a new intimate relationship for a while, although she had made new friends during her recent personal journey.

Angela and Jim were attending a P.A.I.R.S. seminar, which was a long and involved pursuit. The meetings last six or seven months. The results of this investment were obvious to all of us. Angela had gained tremendous insight into her role in the relationship. She had also been showing major strides in self-respect.

"Lately, I figured out that we have, at least I have, a personality or individuality as an adult," Angela said. "But I also have a personality as an adult in an intimate and committed relationship. Different needs and reactions surface as soon as you are a couple, and I am learning to address *my* needs—and his." She was proud to announce what she considers her achievements. She examined the faces around the room and added, "Let me tell you more about it as the seminar progresses."

I could not agree with her more, and I understood her appreciation for the seminar. As much as Angela enjoyed learning from it, I had enjoyed teaching P.A.I.R.S.

Pat had become more comfortable with talking about her attraction to women. She had slowly become more articulate when discussing her sexuality and was now able to be more focused. Sexuality had been a complex topic for her. Now she talked about affection and warm feelings toward one woman in particular—her friend, Heather. We still didn't know much about Heather except that she is gentle, nurturing, and gay. We did know, however, that Pat would not initiate sexual contact in this or any other relationship.

We had watched Pat become more fascinated with the emotional freedom she had been practicing. "Imagine," she said, and her face actually lit up, "having the life you live without an agenda going on in the background. I mean, not having a double life is quite a grand life. You guys should try it. I have no secrets and no tensions. I actually enjoy myself."

Tina moved into the open space in the conversation. "Not having secrets is a novelty for you, but it's not fun for us. And I mean it in the most sexual sense." She giggled.

I picked up Tina's line as if I were given a message to decode, which I often did, both verbal and nonverbal. This time Tina presented me with a relatively easy decoding task. "Well," I said, "I presume it's time to hear from you, Tina, about some sexual secrets."

Tina was surprised. "Who me? Why me? What have I done now?" Her voice was warm without the sarcasm she was known for. She looked pleased that her communication was received.

"I just took a wild guess. Sorry if I made a mistake assuming you have some sexual secrets. I should not have concluded that," I said in mock seriousness. The sweet silence I had intruded on was over, and the room filled with familiar playful energy.

"Well," Tina said, "His name is Jorge. I've never met anyone of the masculine gender with such consideration and kindness. In a man, I mean. Get this, he is romantic and I fell for it. The discovery of romance is not a small thing in my life. Remember me? Ms. Practical Life? Ms. Business All the Time? Well, I am definitely into the romance part of this relationship, and it fits me like a happy fish in water. And I don't think I'll be a sushi!" She added with a grin. We all laughed at her metaphor and marveled that this woman. Ms. Practicality, indeed, looked so much in love.

The women attacked her with questions. Who was Jorge? Where had she met him? What was he like?

Tina held up her hands, laughing. "Okay," she said. "Here it is in some semblance of order. He is a banker; I met him at a charity event. He is Brazilian, and an international banker who has been transferred from Rio. He is your quintessential Latin lover and he is also tall, dark, and very handsome."

"Him being a businessman means you two must have a lot in common," Isabel said facetiously.

"Now don't smirk, Isabel," Tina laughed. "It's true we do have a lot in common, but he is also very different from me."

"How so?" asked Lisa.

"Well, after the charity event, he called me with some information he had promised to get to me. To tell you the truth, I don't even remember asking him for it, but I guess I did." We laughed. "Then he asked me if I liked modern classical music. I said 'I guess so,' not knowing what even constitutes modern classical music. So we made a date. We ended up going to this elegant mansion in Beverly Hills to attend a chamber concert. The music was modern, but one piece was rhythmic, very catchy, as well as being rather atonal.

"There was no program since this was an informal, so-called experimental program, so I asked him afterwards who composed that specific piece that I liked. He looked at me and said simply, 'I did.' Before I could respond, one of the musicians came up to us and thanked Jorge for his work. All I could think was, is my mouth still hanging open?"

We joined in laughter. Pat then pumped her for more information. Tina gladly shared with us the phenomenal sexual world she had discovered. "There are surprises and mysteries everywhere,

Pat. They are different kinds though, all sexual and playful and mischievous in nature. I'm so glad I found out about them," Tina revealed with a big smile.

"Thanks for sharing with us. I'm sure I will feel the same about love when I'm ready. You're a good role model for me, Tina," Pat agreed.

Tina was touched. "Pat, I appreciate you saying that. I never would've thought that you would think of me as a good role model. In fact, I thought you felt the opposite."

"How so?" It was not Pat who jumped in with the question, but Rosie.

Tina gave Rosie an impatient look. "Hey, Rosie, give me some room here. Maybe Pat is not interested in this. Are you, Pat?"

To my surprise, Rosie was not offended. She smiled and shrugged as if to say, "I couldn't help it." She truly could not help it. Rosie is still as impulsive as ever, except now she is not as hypersensitive as she once was. She is willing to see the other person's point of view before she takes it as a personal insult. This time, she just smiled.

"As a matter of fact, I *am* interested," Pat said, bringing the subject back into focus.

Tina was on a roll today and her energy was reflected in her voice. "This was some time ago when I shared with the group my American dream regarding my breasts. Do you recall that time?" she asked.

"We're back to boobs," Lisa giggled. "I was wondering when it would happen. We've spent two weeks without discussing them." She caught us looking at her. "Sorry," she said. "Go ahead. Don't pay any attention to me." She was obviously enjoying this.

"I will, little Lisa, but you listen, too," Tina said. "When I was sharing about my dream, I was trying to say I noticed you, Pat. For some reason, your reaction caught my attention. Despite everything I felt then, I can still see you in my mind's eye." Tina took a long breath, which gave us a minute to switch from the giddy mood to a more therapeutic one.

"I was telling the group about how inadequate my breasts looked to me and how I wanted them to be larger. As I was talking, I noticed that you looked at me with disgust. Pat, this is not a judgment by any means. I just thought that my views were sickening to you."

Pat was listening, but her eyes were downcast. I recalled that Pat had not said a word about Tina's dream when she first told us about it, yet everyone else had expressed their opinions to no end.

Pat volunteered her response without hesitation. "Yes, you're right. I commend you for your acute observation. It started with Lisa and her breast show and continued with you, Tina. And don't let me forget Angela's double breasts. I personally don't like my breasts, and it is a continuous puzzle in my life," she continued.

"You might speculate that I probably have connected my mom's death from breast cancer to my negative relationship with my breasts. You would be correct. I'm terrified of my breasts and I don't enjoy them as a pleasurable organ. For me, breasts represent profound fear. And you, Tina, have mentioned in the past how breasts are coupled with death. Maybe I'm not so different from you in my relationship with my breasts. Yet, I see how Lisa loves her breasts. Beth too. But not me." She had a sad look on her face. The group listened respectfully.

The renewed interest in the subject of breasts did not die with Pat's openness. Beth had been waiting to share some new information and, as it turned out, the subject came up anyway. She told the group about her best friend, Nina, who'd had breast implants about four years ago and was now suffering from some strange collection of symptoms.

"After a series of medical tests and numerous interviews with specialists, it was concluded that Nina was suffering from an immune deficiency disease. I've been her best friend for a long time, and I've never seen her like this. I am disturbed by the entire procedure, by the tests and by the way Nina was treated at the hands of 'experts.' I feel Nina did not get adequate professional attention. It wasn't quick enough nor was any diagnosis clear enough for her to understand, so that she could react appropriately.

"Nina is positive that the disease began after she received the implants," she continued, "and she feels that the implants have caused the disease. She is convinced that the timing is more than coincidental and that her illness is a result of the implants."

Beth has a tendency to repeat herself when she's upset and that was what she was doing at the moment. I identified with her, since I've been accused of acting the same way by my youngest son, Guy.

The group members were interested in the controversy among three of the parties involved: the giant corporations that manufacture the implants, the medical facilities that endorse them, and the legal groups that oppose the implant industry. The controversy piqued a concern for these women from an intellectual point of view, but it resonated with them even more intensely from an emotional place.

As Beth was talking about Nina's circumstances, some women began taking sides and the meeting began to resemble one of our earlier sessions. Grace noted the situation quietly. "I have this feeling I've been there, done that, girls. Are we really going into another round?" She was ignored.

Lisa, Tina, Angela, and Rosie were for the implants. Isabel was happy to endorse them for reconstructive surgery. Jane and Grace were sympathetic about Isabel's predicament and now they were not against implants. Beth was still totally against them. Katherine was neutral. Pat did not want to involve herself in this issue.

Information had been exchanged back and forth: medical evidence, statistics, legal records, newspapers, books, and Web sites. One thing we learned is that even with the growing concern about breast implants, the number of women getting them has reached an all-time high. The number of women having them removed is also at an all-time high. Their reasons range from leakage or other medical complications to feelings of shame for falling prey to society's pressures.

I recalled the case of one of my marital couples. I had not been privy to the fact that Karen had undergone plastic surgery and had breast implants. Karen had recited statistics from the media regarding the dangers of implants. She wanted to have them removed immediately. Her husband did not want her to. Karen was upset and disappointed with his reaction.

Karen protested. "I don't need to be trapped in these. I want to be free of the foreign objects. Listen to the doctors and lawyers on the news! Let me be who I am," she cried. The rest of the session was predictable. The script had been written for them long ago.

Karen held a copy of an article from the Sunday *Washington Post* that a friend had e-mailed to her. She read the last sentence of the article "Popularity of Breast Implants Rising" by Marc Kaufman:

> Women need to know that once they go down the path of having breast implants, their bodies will be changed and there are predictable problems some of them will face.

"Guess what kind of session I had to facilitate last week?" I asked the group. I told them about the woman's predicament and her husband's response.

"I know exactly how she must feel," Angela said. "I'm glad you gave her a voice here, Dr. Nili. I feel the entrapment she is talking about. With all the therapy I'm involved in, I can see clearly now. I went along with my husband's fantasy without even considering the person, the individual that I was. I guess I was not a differentiated individual yet. My husband was severely 'booby-trapped,' but so was I. I don't feel very smart about that part of my life."

"Meaning what?" Lisa asked. She had been protective of Angela ever since we found out about her implants.

"Relax, Lisa. I have no plan. I've a vague wish to remove my implants. I'm sure you can understand me. Don't you?" Angela asked.

There were, no doubt, many women out there who could identify with Angela. We were living in the midst of an enormous wave of women with breast implants who were signing up to have them removed.

Tina had a new reaction. "I am touched by what you've said, Angela. I finally get it. I've always wanted to be busted. My American dream was to have this pair of boobs that would be noticed from afar. But now I don't want to be busted. I mean, the entrapment we were talking about, being caught in the controversy like Nina. Or being afraid of disease like this woman Dr. Nili mentioned. I've never met her, but I feel for her. I'm confused about the role of my breasts in my life."

Beth told us about her impression of Tina's pearl of wisdom. What Beth said only further endeared her to us. She rephrased Tina's statement and said, "Here is what Nina could say: I wanted to be busted, but now I *am* busted!"

The reactions ranged from admiration to concern to empathy. I felt that Tina's confusion was appropriate and timely.

Her contribution regarding feeling busted gained popularity. A week would not go by without someone mentioning the concept, and slowly the expression "busted" spread among the friends and relatives of our group members.

Chapter Twelve

One BREAST at a Time

One Month Later

As any female athlete knows, the larger the breasts the more they interfere with running and jumping. The mythological warriors of ancient Greece, the Amazons, removed their right breasts because they got in the way of their archery.

—from *Survival of the Prettiest,*
by Nancy Etcoff, Ph.D.

The fight to restore the breast's nurturant significance would be taken up at regular intervals during the centuries to come by individuals and groups opposed to the absolute reign of the sexualized breast.

—from *A History of the Breast,*
by Marilyn Yalom

"HERE WE HAVE AN EXAMPLE OF AN INTELLIGENT, EDUCATED, AND attractive young lady who was 'booby-trapped' enough to get into this mess." Beth was holding a well-known women's magazine that featured an article about the implants controversy. The name of the article was telling: "To Implant or Not to Implant." It depicted the suffering of many women and their families, and had printed the corporation's legal arguments on the opposite page. Nina was interviewed for the article, and her picture covered the entire first page of the article. We passed the magazine from hand to hand with great enthusiasm.

Jane said, "This group looks like a bunch of Girl Scouts fighting over the first box of cookies of the season." But her aside was drowned out in the excitement. Jane and I exchanged smiles and were swept into the activity of examining Nina's picture.

"You never told us that she's a fox," Lisa said.

"Nina is one sexy babe," Tina agreed.

"Yes, she is lovely," Beth added, attempting, to no avail, to get the magazine back.

"I thought I'd told you that Nina has everything any young woman would have wished for, plus a terrific sense of humor and a heart of gold." Beth's eyes were tearing up.

Katherine, who was sitting across from Beth, noticed her expression. "What is happening with you, Beth?" It was unusual for us to see Beth like this, and the playful atmosphere was broken as we all turned to her.

She fought back her tears. "I am so frustrated and I feel so helpless," she began. "Nina has hired an attorney. There is a messy trial in the future that will last for years and it will drain her energy. She is weak and unfocused and it's getting worse with all the questioning, the depositions, and the medical tests and checkups."

Angela wanted to say something but caught herself. Jane noticed and pushed her a little. "Go for it, Angela. Don't hold it in," Jane urged.

"Well, Beth, what is it that made you so upset, or annoyed, or disappointed?" There was concern in her voice.

"I'll tell you, Angela, and thank you for your thoughtfulness. Obviously Nina is sick and she is getting sicker. She is not the same joyful human being I've known for years. I feel that everyone takes a chance with every medical procedure. Look at Lisa today. To me she is the best case scenario. She is happy with the results and her health is not threatened.

"The worst case scenario here is Nina who got implants, believing in her surgeon. Now she is sick or believes, psychologically, that she is sick. Then the attorneys forced themselves upon her, showing her how important it is to join with thousands of women in this class action lawsuit against the manufacturers.

"I feel that she got really sick when she signed their contract and started to blame and hate the large corporations. Nina thinks she has hired an attorney to represent her. The truth is that the attorney pursued her relentlessly. He called her and went to her residence numerous times. He pushed her and pushed her. He put her in touch with many other women who were diagnosed with the immune deficiency disease. I went with her to some of their meetings. Nina could not bring herself to drive her car, which she really enjoys doing. I witnessed the process where the attorneys aggressively recruit women dissatisfied with their breast implants. You know how I've advocated against breast implants, so you might think that I like these attorneys." She took a deep breath. Several women were nodding their heads in agreement. Of course it was easy to imagine Beth on the attorneys' side.

"But that's not the case," she continued. She sighed and picked up a tissue. "I'll make it short; the story is already too long. The attorneys and physicians proved to Nina that she, like thousands of other consumers, is sick and will get worse. I don't know how sick she is. I don't know if I believe them. I am sure that a few women are sick, but when I listened to the presentations, I had a feeling they were building a case, and very convincingly so.

"On the one hand, I think Nina is joining them because she is weak physically, and now psychologically she is cooperating and participating in a sort of mass hysteria. On the other hand, if they happen to be right and her immune system is damaged, it's an enormous health problem to face. She is between a rock and a hard place. As you said it, Tina, she is busted."

We knew Beth made sense, since we were well read on the implant controversy. We had no solutions to offer. Removing the implants at this point might not make a difference as the studies showed.

Beth picked up the article with Nina's picture prominently displayed. She looked down at it and said, "This was so unnecessary, Nina. Why did you get yourself into this mess?" She put the magazine away and asked us to go on with the group process.

And the group continued.

In a short time, someone asked about implants and breast-feeding. Katherine said reassuringly, "Again, there are no problems with breast-feeding for a woman with implants."

The conversation turned to breast-feeding in general, which raised both positive and negative memories. Almost every woman had one or two breast-feeding stories.

"There are so many mysteries attached to breast-feeding that I am not sure what to believe," Tina said. "I was breast-fed, but I have no fantasies about feeding a baby who's hanging from my boob."

They also examined the myth of breast size and feeding. Rosie wanted to hear a definite conclusion. "I understand that there is no connection between breast size and the amount of breast milk produced, correct?"

"Absolutely," Jane answered from across the room.

"In the past they used to have a special nanny just for breast-feeding," Rosie said.

"A wet nurse," Jane corrected. "That's what they called her. It was customary in many cultures. The rich used to practice that regularly."

"Borrowed boob service," Tina murmured, but we all heard and laughed.

"I'll share a borrowed boob story," I said, while the laughter lingered. "I heard it from my mom. When I was six months old and still being breast-fed, my mother reported that she had plenty of milk for me. The next-door neighbor had just given birth to a nice-sized baby boy. Baby size was everything, remember? Two days after the neighbor came home from the hospital, she discovered she could not produce enough milk to feed her baby. In no time, the women in the neighborhood became a support group and found two new mothers who were breast-feeding at the time.

"My mom volunteered her breast milk, and twice a day the women would come by and deliver the freshly pumped milk to the neighbor's newborn. My mom was glad she could supply this freshly squeezed liquid gold. I've always felt she is a cool mom."

Jane added, "So it sounds like the women in the neighborhood were practicing the bosom buddies system."

"Indeed," I said. "You might say I learned about bosom buddies from my mother's milk."

Tina chuckled and suggested, "You sure are bonded with this subject. Maybe you should write a book about it."

"Maybe I should. And what would I call this book?"

"The title could be *Squeezing Liquid Gold,*" Tina said. "But if I were the author, my book would be different."

"*Treasured Chest?*" Lisa suggested.

"No," Tina said seriously, "Something like *My Kingdom for Some Breasts.*" And it was obvious that she meant it.

"*All My Breasts.* That's my book," Angela said laughing. This was the first time she had joked about her breasts, and the group applauded her.

"*One Breast at a Time,*" Isabel said cheerfully. We applauded again.

The process amused Beth. *"My Cup Runneth Over,"* she blurted out, thinking, no doubt, about her friendship with her breasts. I got it; she was quoting from Psalms 23. I happened to know that psalm by heart. This quote had nothing to do with the size of her cup. It had to do with Beth's philosophy of life, her feelings of gratitude about life and health.

Katherine's was predictable: *"Mammograms: the Lifesavers."*

"Cup Fear." Pat blurted out, making us groan and laugh as we each picked up on her playful twist with the movie title *Cape Fear.*

Jane was patiently waiting for her turn. She stood up and declared, "My book is unique. It's about the process of unearthing your feelings. It's about a group of women who are yakking about their relationships with their breasts. You'll never guess the title," and she paused. Seeing no takers but expectant faces, she said, "I'd call it *Off Your Chest.* It will definitely be a best seller." The group applauded, and then gave her a standing ovation. The noise was tremendous.

Rosie took her time and, pointing at Lisa, said, *"Do Blondes' Breasts Have More Fun?"* The laughter grew louder, understanding Rosie's preoccupation with Lisa.

Grace, though, was not in a jolly mood. Beth nudged her. "C'mon. What would your book be called, Grace?" Beth asked.

Grace raised her arm as if to push Beth, then stopped. She looked around the room. Tears were in her eyes. She took a deep breath and sighed. Finally, she stretched her arms out to us and a slight shriek came out of her, *"Feed Me."* Then she exploded, her words tumbling out. "My book is about the secret of human milk. A book about selfless nurturing. About the human milk of kindness. The act of giving of yourself, feeding from yourself. You know, being human." For Grace, this was both personal and generational. She looked down on Amy's decision not to breast-feed as selfish.

Amy's refusal to breast-feed was not a rarity. Each one of us had brought in many examples of friends and relatives who, for one reason or another, had not breast-fed their newborns. Amy clearly had definite opinions about breast-feeding. Those opinions were personal and not for us to judge.

Grace studied Lisa. "The human body is not a sacred object you should worship. The human soul is sacred and so is human life. Your breasts are not a religion or a philosophy you have to believe in. Feeding an infant is by itself not a sacred act, but it does feel spiritual to a mother, to the infant, and also to the father who is watching. There are a few more values I taught my kids. Honesty and doing the right thing in life are great values; loving others is another one. Fidelity in marriage is a good value, and there are many more. These are the values I instilled in my kids. Amy, though, believes in other things."

"What does she believe in?" Katherine asked. The group listened respectfully.

"My Amy? She believes in what she reads in the women's magazines. But especially she believes in the mirror." Grace's eyes were still fixed on Lisa who shifted uneasily in her seat.

"I'm aware, Lisa, that I make you uncomfortable. I don't mean to hurt you, I am investing in you, too, when I spill my guts about Amy. If I cannot help her, maybe I can help you. In the meantime, I feel like I have failed motherhood. I cannot, for the life of me, teach my own flesh and blood some normal and natural mothering. For heaven's sake, what is going on in her head?" This was not the first time we heard about Amy's philosophy, but to see Grace's desperation about it was very touching.

Lisa did not resent Grace's outburst. She looked at her, speechless. That was a rarity. Lisa swallowed, a symbolic gesture that she was taking in what was said. Finally she said, slowly, "I had never looked at it that way."

I had no idea what she meant. I waited.

"I don't know what's on Amy's mind," Lisa said. "Now I know I have been ashamed of my body for as long as I can remember."

She looked around at us. "How many of you have tasted what shame feels like?" she asked.

"Tina, you've felt inadequate. That means to me you've felt that you're not good enough. Maybe it's bordering on shame.

"Angela, my angel, you've felt shame. Not for those small boobs, but you've felt it about the new ones, the double breasts story.

"Pat, when you speak about your tits, I don't hear shame. I hear fear. Big time. And you are not free of it even now.

"And the rest of you, you don't know what shame feels like. I have a feeling that Rosie does. Am I right? And so do Nina and Amy.

"People, don't be so quick to judge. Live in my bra for a few days. Like, walk in my shoes, you know what I mean. Give us a break. Us, the shamed girls, women, whatever." She stopped and took a deep breath.

Lisa opened up to us on an emotional level that we had not heard before. She was sincere, honest, and not looking for applause. She was real. Lisa did not look like a cheerleader any longer. She looked like a woman. A beautiful young lady who owns her feelings and knows who she is.

Her declaration of shame was an intense emotional experience for Rosie, who was crying quietly.

Grace clutched the tissue box and sat still, a look of complete surprise frozen on her face.

Isabel got up and went over to Lisa, then gave her a long hug. Lisa responded and hugged her back. They stood there for a few seconds. Then Isabel stepped back, smiled, and said, "I've never heard you speak like that. Your depth of feeling and your understanding of others show a lot of growth."

Lisa beamed, obviously enjoying the positive feedback. "I know I've not said those things before, but since your surgery, Isabel—no, since your diagnosis—I've been having lots of new feelings." Lisa indeed looked more mature. She turned toward Grace. Everyone was on the edge of her seat. "Grace, I appreciate the investment you make in me. I do get it. I've been here all along and I have been listening. I have received wonderful things from all of you. I owe you. In many respects, your attention is what I've been craving forever. My mom was too busy to notice my needs. You guys represent what I missed. For me, you are my mother's milk." Grace's face radiated tenderness.

Angela said softly, "Thank you, Lisa. We do nurture you with our love." Grace nodded with agreement.

Lisa acknowledged it and continued, "I have some more to share. I'm in a fine relationship with Jeff. I am growing in leaps and bounds. Jeff is talking about forever. He wants a future with me—marriage—and he would like to raise a family. Not immediately but sometime in the future. Can you believe it? Of course you can. You guys have the right ideas about relationships.

"And now to you, Grace. Thanks to your guidance, I got a glimpse of the importance of breast-feeding. I know you're surprised, but I do have fantasies about family life, babies, and, yes, feeding my baby with my own breasts. Don't faint here. I know it took forever but I finally got it." Lisa stopped for a second and took a long breath.

"But now, Grace, I want to give you a treasure similar to the one you gave me," Lisa continued. "I want to show you that what Amy is saying is a coded message. Ask Dr. Nili to decode it for you. I can feel Amy. Be patient with her. I've been there, as you know. That's why you were talking directly to me. I hope you can see that I'm in a new place now. And I know you will be happy for me." Lisa was finished. It had been a mouthful. Her philosophy had turned around completely. It was a transformation that no one had predicted.

The women were looking at me, but Grace's look was the most intense.

"What coded behavior does Lisa mean? Help me here," she asked.

"It's not a mystery, Grace," I said. "You've actually said it before. Amy wants to stay a teenager. Well, it's not about being a teenager really. It's a message from Amy. Simply stated, I don't want adult responsibilities. I want to stay young without a child hanging all over me, sucking my life away."

"This is a lot to think about," Grace said. She was sitting up straight, with tears streaming down her face. "It fits perfectly with what Amy has been saying all along. She's not ready. Her husband, Josh, *is* ready. Amy is *not*." She turned to Lisa and said simply, gratefully, "Thank you, Lisa."

"You are totally welcome," Lisa smiled. She reached into her bag with both hands and pulled out a wrapped package. With fast hand movements, she removed the wrappings, then lifted her hands for us to see. Up in the air was a new tissue box. Lisa circled the room showing us the box. "This is my gift to this group. A small addition to the collection. I thank you all."

The tissue box had an illustration around it—the famous nudes *The Three Graces* by Peter Paul Rubens. Of course.

The women's psychotherapy group was coming to an end. Our allotted time together was long past. Officially, the group ended when Isabel had been diagnosed with breast cancer. But the women had unanimously decided to continue to meet regularly until we were comfortable with Isabel's recovery.

There was no graduation ceremony. There was, however, a chance to reflect on the journey we had traveled together.

Each woman had entered the group process booby-trapped to a different degree. Isabel, perhaps the least booby-trapped, had developed an even healthier, internally connected relationship with her own breasts. Unfortunately, she had to fight breast cancer to achieve it. The group watched with admiration how she gracefully accepted her now healthy breasts and her new life. In the process, she learned about her inability to connect with her husband.

In the last sessions as the divorce had been initiated, Isabel made a brilliant connection for further understanding her part in her marriage to Peter. She had figured out that her expectations of marriage were similar to what she had experienced at home growing up. Her father traveled the world as a diplomat while her mom was home raising the family and hosting the active social life to which they were accustomed. Similar to Isabel's marriage, there was not much intimacy. The females of the family hung out together and looked out for each other. Isabel realized that only after Peter had been diagnosed with his sexual addiction disorder. Now, she's on a new journey of discovering her needs for true intimate relationships.

Lisa made an exclusive commitment to Jeff, and they promised to both work on their expectations of each other. Lisa, who was extremely booby-trapped at the onset of this group, had evolved greatly. Now she is primarily interested in developing and maintaining an intimate relationship and is less concerned with the reactions she gets to her newly enhanced breasts.

Rosie used the group process to her benefit, but she was the one member who grew mainly from listening and taking in the other women's evolving awareness. She chose from each one, selecting what would best be a new representation for her. She actually internalized many of the lessons and developed a firm sense of self as well as appeared less envious of others.

Pat had a breakthrough. She continued her friendship with Heather, and with Heather's help, had her first sexual encounter with a woman lover. She was happy to report to the group that it was "an amazing emotional experience." She had even developed a sense of humor about it. She told the group that being involved sexually with a woman was sweet and tender and very nurturing. Then she casually added with a sly glance at Angela, "There were so many boobs to worry about."

Grace uncovered her dynamics with her late husband, which had been brewing for several sessions. Grace had not admitted to herself the severity of his gambling addiction. Just as in Isabel and Pat's cases, the truth was always there. She was finally able to look at the gambling from its ugliest side. Just before he died, they lost their house. Grace had to survive without her spouse *and* her own home. Her trauma had been doubled. Later, she had to declare bankruptcy and learn new ways of living.

Grace's relationship with her breasts was functional. She was clear about their purpose and enjoyed the bond her breasts enabled her to create with her children in their infancy. Erroneously, she felt that the breast-feeding bond was strong enough to last forever. Breast-feeding was important to her, and therefore she gave no importance to the size or shape of women's breasts.

Beth had entered our group free of booby traps. She was a mature model for the other women on issues of self-acceptance. Her relationship with Nina has continued, but Nina was never the same again. Throughout their friendship, Nina found ways to slow the pace of her daily life. Beth, on the other hand, gave Nina a great deal of nurturing. For Beth, this was a natural development since she liked to invest her caring in the people around her.

Angela was still working on her marriage. Some time earlier, she mentioned she wanted to remove her implants when Beth brought in information about the class action lawsuit. Angela was firm even after a medical checkup found the implants to be safe. She took full responsibility for her part in deciding to have the implants put in, so this was a positive development toward her personal growth. The "poor girl versus the bad husband" was no longer the issue. She rejected the victim position. Her relationship at home grew to be affectionate and caring. Now Angela has decided to keep her "double breasts" and is moving away from a booby-trapped life towards greater freedom.

Katherine was moving out of her clinical cage. She realized that in the extreme lifestyle she was leading, she was missing social involvement and fun. She started to date and soon declared she was in love with Tom, an easygoing TV writer who moved to L.A.

after graduating from college in Wisconsin. They met at the clinic where they both were volunteering: Katherine was practicing medicine and Tom was practicing one-liners with the kids who came in for their medications.

Katherine, who was not booby-trapped, had not been able to experience much pleasure through her body. But even her breasts "were rejoicing" now, she confessed to us with surprise in her voice. Grinning, she said that now "there is a lot of pleasure on my chest."

Jane was slow to grow emotionally. She had been highly opinionated all along, and she was not in the habit of opening up to others, a posture she maintained throughout the group experience. Still, she was a highly sociable person who simply does not like to disclose much unless she is in crisis. From time to time, we had encouraged Jane to work harder on some issues, but, being a strong-willed person, she had fought us tooth and nail. Jane would have grown more working one-on-one with a therapist so that she could not hide behind other people's needs. When I recommended a therapist for her, to my surprise she agreed and contacted the person.

Jane was the only group member who did not want to terminate the group. She pleaded with us to continue the meetings. At the last group session, she reported that her first individual session had gone fine. When I looked pleased, she added, "I think I have a couple of ideas for helping my new therapist get more patients." If I am not mistaken, Jane was simply resisting and digging in her heels deeper. The therapist she was referred to, however, is highly qualified and will undoubtedly see her through her resistance.

Tina came into the group severely booby-trapped. She had tried hard to see others' points of view on issues of intimacy, sexuality, health, and especially self-esteem. She had to unlearn in a relatively short time some myths she had been carrying with her since childhood. She also needed to adjust to the real value of a sensuous human body. It was a struggle for her to integrate such a concept into her thinking, given that she was obsessed with her American dream to have large breasts. It was fascinating to watch her personal growth. Since her divorce, she had dated occasionally without excitement or commitment. But as soon as Tina experienced the smallest steps toward self-acceptance, her relationships gained more meaning. They led her to being able to open up to Jorge and the quiet joy that he brought her.

This major change happened when Tina witnessed Isabel going through the trauma of breast cancer. Immediately after the surgery, Tina let go of her American dream. One day, she read us a paragraph from the book *Bosom Buddies* about the new statistics regarding Japanese women who immigrated to the United States and the increased number of breast cancer cases among them. In our last session, Tina said this statistic had been on her mind constantly. "My American dream turned into a form of an American nightmare. I used to think of living here in America as being close to my promised land, my land of milk and honey. But I'm giving up on the land of milk. Now I want to be with my honey. I want to be in this loving relationship for a long time—not with my boobs, mind you, but with my real honey, this man who loves me totally and equally."

Chapter Thirteen

Treasured CHEST™

A Personal Workbook

At some point, our breasts will shape how we look at the world, and how the world looks back at us.

—from *Breasts,* by Meema Spadola

Forming loving relationships that nurture us, and nurturing ourselves directly through the choices we make about how we live our lives, can help us to create breast health.

—from *The Wisdom of Menopause,*
by Christiane Northrup, M.D.

THE HONESTY OF THE WOMEN IN THIS GROUP AND THEIR evolution toward being less booby-trapped was my inspiration for creating "Treasured Chest," the first relationship guide to a woman's breasts. You may read and write in it in increments, one part at a time, or straight through.

You can use the guide as a personal workbook. The activities in "Treasured Chest" are designed to evoke memories and make you aware of several important issues. Because it is a personal experience, some privacy should be exercised until the time you are ready to share.

Think about the questions.

Go in your mind back to your personal experiences.

Answer the questions for yourself first before you ask another woman.

Create Bosom Buddies groups in your geographical or *virtual* communities.

Share the information with other women in your life.

Encourage the women you care about to live free of a booby-trapped life.

Discover the feelings of Treasured Chest, individually and in groups.

When you come across a memory or story about breasts that you want to share with the rest of the Bosom Buddies groups, please e-mail it through a link you'll find on my Web site at www.boobytrapped.com.

Treasured Chest: *A Personal Workbook*

1.

The Quiz

2.

My Mother's Breasts

3.

The New Language for Breasts

4.

Myths and Realities about Breasts

5.

The Feeding Breasts

6.

Budding

7.

Bravo Bra

8.

My Breasts and Me

9.

Double-Breasted

10.

Breasts and Fears

11.

Be Your Own Sex Therapist

12.

Breast Cancer Survivors

13.

The Augmented Breasts

14.

The Quiz, Again

15.

A Daily Breasts Meditation

PART 1. THE QUIZ

ARE YOU BOOBY-TRAPPED?

Answer each of the following questions with *yes* or *no*. (Men, please answer for a wife, significant other, daughter, or sister.)

1. My mother has never shared with me her attitude about her own breasts.

    ❏ YES   ❏ NO

2. Watching breast-feeding in public is shameful and makes me uncomfortable.

    ❏ YES   ❏ NO

3. When in the presence of a woman, I am embarrassed when I am conscious of her breasts.

    ❏ YES   ❏ NO

4. I have never had a relationship with my breasts that I am aware of.

    ❏ YES   ❏ NO

5. I spend more time thinking about my hair, skin, nails, and heart than on the health of my breasts.

    ❏ YES   ❏ NO

6. I never respond in any way when I touch my breasts.

    ❏ YES   ❏ NO

7. Large-breasted women are more sexually responsive than small-breasted women.

❏ YES   ❏ NO

8. It is true that a woman's breast size correlates to her mothering abilities.

❏ YES   ❏ NO

9. Sagging breasts are a sign of diminished sexual excitement for a woman.

❏ YES   ❏ NO

10. I have sometimes been envious or obsessed with another woman's breasts.

❏ YES   ❏ NO

KEY

Count the number of times you answered YES. Here's how you rate:

0–2: Congratulations! You are booby-trapped-free. Keep it up.

3–4: You are somewhat booby-trapped. You need to improve your attitude.

5–7: Rethink your value system. You are potentially hurtful to others.

8–10: You are severely booby-trapped. Get help now!

PART 2. MY MOTHER'S BREASTS

Beth, a character in *Booby-Trapped*, who has a clear and healthy relationship with her breasts, inspired this part about mother's breasts. She told us stories about various breasts in her family. Here's a story about her grandmother.

> My late grandmother's breasts were considered to be enormous in size. We witnessed several anecdotes regarding her breasts' size and shape. One time my grandmother and I were kibitzing in the living room when my mother called out for us. Our lemon tea and cake were ready to be served. My grandmother answered my mother, saying "Honey, I don't need to come to the table in the dining room for a snack. Look, I'll just unfold my napkin and put it all over my chest, so I can use it as a table." She proceeded to spread the napkin over her large breasts and placed the saucer on it. She put the teacup on the saucer, dropped in two sugar cubes, and looked around the room proudly as she stirred her tea.

1. Do you remember your mother's breasts? _____
    _____
    _____
    _____
    _____

2. What was your first memory of them? _____
    _____
    _____
    _____
    _____

3. How did they look?_____

    _____

    _____

    _____

    _____

4. How did they feel to your touch?_____

    _____

    _____

    _____

    _____

5. What kind of texture did they have? _____

    _____

    _____

    _____

    _____

6. What kind of scent did they have? _____

    _____

    _____

    _____

    _____

7. Have you ever smelled that scent again? _____

    _____

    _____

    _____

    _____

8. When was the last time you saw your mother's breasts? ___

    _____

    _____

    _____

    _____

9. Did your mother ever share with you her attitudes about her own breasts? If so, what were they? _____

    _____

    _____

    _____

    _____

10. Are there any stories, anecdotes, or rituals in your family about older generations' relationships or attitudes toward their breasts? What are they? _____

    _____

    _____

    _____

    _____

11. Now, draw a picture of your mother's breasts.

PART 3.
THE NEW LANGUAGE FOR BREASTS

Jane, another character from *Booby-Trapped*, kept a close count of all new terms and language regarding breasts. Jane insisted that we use these terms to convey specific attitudes. This part was her idea. It will provide an opportunity to develop new attitudes about our breasts—a new language for you to use.

A. BOOBY-TRAPPED

Booby-Trapped is a point of view, a mind-set.

It is also the range of attitudes from a preoccupation with females' breasts to an obsession with them.

Many women pay a great deal of attention to the size and shape of their own breasts. They compare themselves to others and feel inferior. Some women even hate their breasts; they wish for larger breasts, or smaller ones, or perkier ones. Those women are booby-trapped.

Men who wish that their mates had different breasts are also booby-trapped. Beliefs of their husbands—and other male friends—play a major part in the attitudes women form about their own breasts. Indeed, some of the women who inspired this workbook had literally fallen into this "man-made" trap.

Women may be echoing what they hear or sense from men, but men may also be echoing what they hear or sense from women. The experience of being booby-trapped has become deep and wide in our North American culture.

To attach importance to only one body part and make women feel diminished because of its natural development is morally wrong. Yet, this entrapment has spread down through the last two generations; mothers have passed it on to their daughters.

Anyone—man or woman, or even an entire society—can be booby-trapped. In our culture, small breasts are belittled; in Brazil, they used to be praised. In several tribes in the world breasts are not an issue.

Examine your attitudes now and determine if you are or to what extent you are booby-trapped. Doing that is the first positive step toward an emotional self-examination of your relationship with your breasts.

How do we know if a person is booby-trapped?

Examples:

- When the other person in a conversation with you is repeatedly fixing their eyes on your breasts rather than on your eyes...Your partner is booby-trapped!
- When describing a female to others, the speaker begins the description with the size or shape of that female's breasts...He or she is booby-trapped!
- If a woman criticizes the size of her own bust, or compares her size to others' with pride or envy...She is booby-trapped!
- When a woman expects the enhancement of her breasts size to bring her inner peace, happiness, or even the right man for marriage...She is booby-trapped!

B. DOUBLED-BREASTED

Double-Breasted is a state of mind that has been known to most women, but not to men. Well, the secret is out.

It has been my clinical observation that most females, even before their breasts begin to develop, have an idea in mind of what their breasts should be. Too often, though, what emerges in reality does not fit our fantasy. Therefore, we hold in our minds an image of an ideal breast, just as we carry on our person our reality. This process is normal and necessary for the young, developing and budding girls.

As growing females we are, in a phrase, double-breasted, and we have a hard time reconciling the two. Maturity, positive experiences as females and a balanced support system may help, and eventually should reconcile our fantasy with our reality. In the best case scenario, we'll accept the reality of our physical breasts. Thus, the phenomenon of being double-breasted is temporary and age appropriate. Or so I wish.

Many women I have met and interviewed are ambivalent about their relationship with their breasts. Even the women who liked their breasts in their youth, are mourning the "loss" of the look and vitality of their breasts.

Like the permanency of one's height and the color of one's eyes, so is the size and shape of one's breasts. There was never room for negotiation. Until now.

We treat our breasts—the ones we do not like—as foreign objects. Unfortunately, society is only too happy to play along with our frustrations. Men's magazines and Madison Avenue advertising tell us that it is chic, acceptable, to have larger ones, smaller ones, perkier ones, symmetrical ones.

What I discovered that was new was the amount of time, effort, and mental anguish many women spend "dealing" with their breasts. I also found an increasing number of women practicing a variation on the subject of self-blame: blaming their breasts—the shapes and sizes—for what was not working in their lives.

Women like Tina, Lisa, Rosie, and Amy showed symptoms of being emotionally stuck. Instead of addressing their issues, they were quick to blame it on the size and shape of their breasts, mirroring what millions of women are feeling. They are Double-Breasted, having a negative relationship with their real breasts while fantasizing about an ideal pair.

How can you tell if a woman is double–breasted? Examples:

- She often mentions the "glory" of her breasts in her youth.
- She is disappointed with the size and/or shape of her breasts now versus her expectations, hopes, or plans.

C. BOSOM BUDDIES

While Booby-Trapped and Double-Breasted are the problems, Bosom Buddies is part of the solution!

An example of how the Bosom Buddies system works was demonstrated with this group of women. To help them in their evolution, they decided to stay after each session and have an intimate discussion on issues and attitudes related to breasts—anybody's breasts.

The women shared stories that had been passed down through their families for generations. They were interested in breast health, both physically and psychologically. The meetings developed into a support group. Slowly, the intimacy of such meetings grew into a system not only of shared memories but also reassurances, including regular self-examinations. One of the best parts of the Bosom Buddies system has been keeping track of mammogram checkups and making sure each group member kept her appointment. Sometimes they would accompany each other to such appointments.

Moreover, the group has been so happy with the Bosom Buddies system that the women have taken it one step further. Most of them have created another group in their neighborhoods, or circle of friends, or with other female members of their families, with one goal in mind: to evoke an awareness of how to develop a healthy relationship with their breasts.

An idea that developed lately came from groups that met in the neighborhood near their homes or workplaces. Some women wanted to exchange their feelings and thoughts with other women from across the country. Well, in no time and with little effort, several virtual groups became Bosom Buddies. They enter their chat rooms and find information, education, and comfort in each other's support.

Now, that is a fine example of the Bosom Buddies system!

D. TREASURED CHEST

Another solution for being Booby-Trapped and Double-Breasted is a journey of discovery. Breasts may be vulnerable to cancer. The fact that your breasts are healthy now may and should be a great source of pleasure and gratitude.

Using your personal workbook, you may seek to change some negative attitudes to positive ones. Here is a practical way to overcome being Booby-Trapped and Double-Breasted.

Your ability to distinguish between health and fashion will free you to experience your own Treasured Chest. You too can learn self-acceptance and develop an affirmative relationship with your breasts.

Treasured Chest is a mental and spiritual journey of discovering the heritage and roots of femininity in you.

Here is the first lesson in recognizing the treasure you carry on your body:

**Size and Shape are Human Tissues,
Shame and Fear are Human Issues!**

PART 4. MYTHS AND REALITIES ABOUT BREASTS

Katherine, whose energy and knowledge was invested in health and prevention, was a major contributor to the following part.

1. Have you ever thought that large-breasted women were more attractive than small-breasted ones? (Please explain your answers to all parts of this question.) _____

_____

_____

Sexier? _____

_____

_____

_____

More sexually available or "loose"? _____

_____

_____

_____

More sexually responsive? _____

_____

_____

_____

More sexually active? _____

_____

_____

_____

Other? _____

_____

_____

_____

2. What is the connection, if any, between breast size and the ability to breast-feed? _____

    _____

    _____

    _____

    _____

    _____

3. Is there a correlation between a woman's breast size and her maternal instinct? Explain. _____

    _____

    _____

    _____

    _____

    _____

4. Do women in general have a positive attitude toward their own breasts? _____

    _____

    _____

    _____

    _____

    _____

5. Does hair growing around the areola mean anything about a woman's sexuality? Femininity? Sensuality? Heredity? _____

    _____

    _____

    _____

    _____

    _____

6.   Are sagging or drooping breasts a sign of lesser sexual excitement for that woman? No excitement? _____

   _____

   _____

   _____

   _____

7.   Do you think that breast-feeding will ruin a woman's looks?

   _____

   _____

   _____

   _____

8.   Do all men love women's breasts? _____

   _____

   _____

   _____

   _____

9.   Are all men obsessed with breasts? _____

   _____

   _____

   _____

   _____

10.   Besides love, what other emotions do you think men express about women's breasts? (For example, ownership.)

   _____

   _____

   _____

   _____

PART 5. THE FEEDING BREASTS

Grace had been very clear about breasts' main function: feeding infants. She called it a "human act of giving."

1. Were you breast-fed? _____

    _____

    _____

    a. If not, why not? _____

    _____

    _____

    b. If yes, until what age? Why? _____

    _____

    _____

    c. If yes, were you breast-fed by your own mother? _____

    _____

    _____

2. What were you told about that experience? _____

    _____

    _____

    _____

3. What is your impression of your mother's breast-feeding experiences with you? _____

    _____

    _____

    _____

4. What do you think it was like for your mom? _____

    _____

    _____

    _____

5. Was there ever a mention of the quantity of breast milk available? _____

_____

_____

_____

6. Was there a story or memory about lack of milk? Overflow?

_____

_____

_____

7. Have you ever seen a mother breast-feeding in public?

_____

_____

_____

8. How do you feel about breast-feeding in public? Does it make you uncomfortable? Threatened? Shameful? _____

_____

_____

_____

9. Do you wish that your mate would not notice women breast-feeding in public? And if so, why? _____

_____

_____

_____

10. Should there be a law against women breast-feeding in public?_____

_____

_____

_____

11. Have you ever seen another woman's breasts when she was breast-feeding? _____

_____

_____

_____

_____

12. Do you consider feeding breasts attractive? Unattractive?

_____

_____

_____

_____

13. Have you noticed any difference in the look of a woman's breasts who breast-fed and one who had never done so? If you answered yes, what was the difference? _____

_____

_____

_____

_____

14. Are you aware of any incidents or stories regarding your infancy and breast-feeding? Your siblings? Your children?

_____

_____

_____

_____

15. Here is Grace's story about her daughter and son-in-law, Amy and Josh. Amy has just told her husband that she would not consider breast-feeding.

> Lately, I found out that Amy and Josh had this huge fight. Apparently, Josh is the one who wants children soon. He wants to participate in raising them, you know, like so many young fathers today. He actually wants to be an equal caretaker since he is home most days. He finally sat Amy down and they really talked it through. Josh found out from Amy that she had made a decision never to breast-feed her babies. She does not want her breasts to be ruined. She wants them to be perky forever, she said. I'd never known this about her. Josh is so beside himself. He cannot believe that his own kids will not be breast-fed. He is into health foods, yoga, mental health, you know. During their fight—which is what it became—they mentioned getting a divorce. I am dying inside. Don't we know what they are made for? Our breasts were put on earth for the purpose of breast-feeding, not breast-dancing or breast-parading. They're not status symbols. They're not just there to tell the difference between men and women. They're a genetic disposition.

What is your reaction to Grace's ideas? _____

_____
_____
_____
_____
_____
_____
_____

16. Are you familiar with your family stories and traditions about breast-feeding? Please write down those anecdotes. And give the stories names! _____

_____

_____

_____

_____

_____

_____

17. Dr. Christiane Northrup, in her extensive and informative book *Women's Bodies, Women's Wisdom,* writes:

> In a culture in which women and men alike are brought up on Barbie dolls, Miss America pageants, and Playboy images, breasts are a very charged part of our anatomy, both physically and metaphorically.

Later in her book she makes another interesting comment:

> I believe many people when they were children didn't get nearly the ideal amount of contact with mothers' breast; too many of us have been nurtured not by maternal breasts but by cold, plastic nipples and chemical formula made by multinational corporations. No wonder our society is hung up on the female breast! No wonder the stage gets set so early for distress in this area of the female body!

What is your reaction to this excerpt? _____

_____

_____

_____

_____

_____

_____

18.	In her excellent book *Survival of the Prettiest*, Dr. Nancy Etcoff has a line in the chapter named "Size Matters":

> Men will see breasts as sexier the less they remind them of feeding stations.

What do you think of that? _____

_____

_____

_____

_____

_____

_____

19.	Here is a mouthful of an idea: In her book *Woman, An Intimate Geography*, Natalie Angier concludes her chapter on breast milk this way:

> In the real world of two-career family, most women will breast-feed for the first few weeks or months of their baby's life, and then they will supplement or replace breast milk with formula. Like women throughout history, they will do the best they can under the constraints of work, duty, and desire. They will be generous and selfish, mammals and magicians, and they will flow and stop flowing. Whatever they do, they will feel guilty for not doing enough.

What are your thoughts? _____

_____

_____

_____

_____

_____

_____

PART 6. BUDDING

Rosie, who has never liked her body, was especially traumatized when her breasts were budding. She would have appreciated the following lesson as a child.

I found this charming short story in the book *I'm on My Way Running: Women Speaking on Coming of Age*. The story is called The Brassiere, by Paul Fournel. It takes place in France. Adeline, a young girl, is raised in a religious atmosphere. Her grandmother bought her first bra and brought it home to her.

> Adeline pulled off her sweater and looked at her breasts. For some time the nipples had been red and swollen; they stuck out a good half-inch from her ribs. She took the bra out of the paper bag. It bore as little resemblance as possible to the provocative strapless brassieres that she saw in the magazines, but it was a bra all right.

As the story continues, Adeline examines the bra and tries it on. She moves her arms, back, and shoulders in an attempt to see if her breasts will move with the rest of her. Then comes the moment of truth, when her girlfriends notice that she is wearing a bra. The girls make some jokes and experiment with the bra as a new toy, including touching Adeline when she has the bra on, which disturbs her. She is afraid she has sinned, doing something unspeakable.

> For twenty days and twenty nights, she held out and never took off her brassiere. She washed through the gaps. It grew dull, it became dirty. The twenty-first morning her grandmother became aware of the situation, got angry, and scolded her. Adeline was severely punished and immediately felt better.

1. When did you first notice your breasts beginning to develop?

    _____

    _____

    _____

2. Do you remember the experience as too soon for you? Too late? _____

    _____

    _____

    _____

3. Did you have a "role model" for your breast development? If so, was she mother, grandmother, sister, aunt, or friend?

    _____

    _____

    _____

    _____

4. Were you ever told by an adult that your breasts would develop to a certain shape or size? If so, who told you?

    _____

    _____

    _____

    _____

5. And then what actually happened? _____

    _____

    _____

    _____

6. Did you wear a training bra? _____

    _____

    _____

    _____

7. Looking back, what did you feel when you first began developing breasts? _____

    _____

    _____

    _____

8. Were you self-conscious when you began developing?

    _____

    _____

    _____

    _____

9. As your breasts began to develop, was one of them bigger than the other? If so, which one? _____

    _____

    _____

    _____

10. Are your breasts now of equal size? If not, have they changed? Is the bigger one now the smaller? _____

    _____

    _____

    _____

    _____

11. Imagine that you are the parent of a fifteen-year-old girl who has developed relatively small breasts. Two of her classmates are planning to have breast implants, with their parents' consent. Your daughter wants to have implants too. How do you respond? _____

    _____

    _____

    _____

    _____

12.   In her book *Dr. Susan Love's Breast Book,* Dr. Love writes:

> Breast size has nothing to do with capacity to make milk, or with vulnerability to cancer or other breast disease. Very large breasts, however, can be physically uncomfortable, and, like very small or uneven breasts, they can be emotionally uncomfortable as well. Often there is a ridge of fat at the bottom of the breast. This 'infra-mammary ridge' is normal, the result of our breasts folding over themselves because we walk upright. Many women find that their nipples don't face front; they stick out slightly toward the armpit. There's a reason for this. Picture yourself holding the baby you are about to nurse. The baby's head is held in the crook of your arm—a nipple pointing to the side is comfortably close to the baby's mouth.

What is your reaction to this excerpt? _____

_____

_____

_____

_____

_____

_____

_____

_____

_____

_____

_____

_____

_____

_____

PART 7. BRAVO BRA

Tina's American dream was to fill up a bra two sizes larger than her breasts. Tina has since let go of her dream.

According to the Nutritional Research Foundation, many women wear ill-fitting bras that give little or no support or that redirect the breast tissue, impeding circulation and lymphatic drainage.

In a 1999 Minneapolis *Star Tribune* article, Christi Mays writes:

> If your bra slips, slides, or sags, causing you to bounce and bulge, you are probably one of the 85 out of 100 women wearing the wrong bra size. Many women squeeze themselves into a bra that is too small, thinking that going up a size is a sign of gaining weight.
>
> For a proper fit, the bottom of the bra should fit the rib cage, not the breasts. In the back, the bra should come down below the shoulder blades. All the breast tissues should be contained inside the cup and the bra should hold the breasts firm with no or little give when you jump in the air. The bust should be supported from underneath the breast, not from the shoulders.

1.   Who decided when it was time for you to wear a bra? ____

_____

_____

_____

_____

2.   Was the timing correct? _____

_____

_____

_____

3. Were there any traditions or rituals in your family about buying a girl's first bra? _____

_____

What was your first bra like? _____

_____

Make? _____

_____

Shape? _____

_____

Style? _____

_____

Color? _____

_____

Texture? _____

_____

Size? _____

_____

Smell? _____

_____

4. What was it like to feel that first bra against your skin? Strange? Restricting? A sense of freedom? A burden? Celebration? Fear? Other? _____

_____

_____

_____

5. Have your initial feelings about wearing a bra changed? If so, how? _____

_____

_____

_____

6. Did you have to explain to other girls about wearing a bra? How was the experience? _____

_____

_____

_____

_____

7. As an adult, have you known women who have "special feelings" for bras? An obsession? Collect them? _____

_____

_____

_____

_____

8. Do you have a favorite bra? Are you wearing it right now?

_____

_____

_____

_____

9. How do you determine what bra to wear and when? _____

_____

_____

_____

_____

10. Do you go bra shopping alone or with someone else? ____

_____

_____

_____

_____

11. Are bras a subject of discussions with your friends? Family?

     _____

     _____

     _____

     _____

12. If a bra is your size, does that mean it will fit? _____

     _____

     _____

     _____

     _____

13. Do you have "trenches" in your shoulders where your bra
     has been digging in? What are you going to do about it?

     _____

     _____

     _____

     _____

14. Do you wear a certain bra for a certain mood? Or does
     wearing a certain bra give you a certain feeling? _____

     _____

     _____

     _____

     _____

PART 8. MY BREASTS AND ME

Isabel had a positive relationship with her breasts, and in spite of her struggle with breast cancer, her attitude became an inspiration to us all.

1. How many names do you know for women's breasts? ____

    _____
    _____
    _____
    _____

2. Rank these terms from the "most comfortable" to the "least comfortable." _____

    _____
    _____
    _____
    _____

3. What is the reason for the most comfortable name? _____

    _____
    _____
    _____
    _____

4. What is the reason for the least comfortable name? _____

    _____
    _____
    _____
    _____

5. Do you have a relationship with your breasts that you are aware of? _____

_____

_____

_____

_____

6. Do you spend as much time and energy on your breasts as you would on your hair, for example? If yes, describe how you treat them. If not, explain. _____

_____

_____

_____

_____

7. Do you ever treat your breasts in any special way? How?

_____

_____

_____

_____

8. Have you developed any distinct feelings toward your breasts such as love? Anger? Disappointment? Pride? Shame? Indifference? Hate? Wonder? Hope? Others? _____

_____

_____

_____

_____

9. Are you clear or confused about the feelings you have about your breasts? _____

_____

_____

_____

10. How do your breasts feel when you touch them? _____

_____

_____

_____

_____

11. What is it like for your hands to touch your breasts? _____

_____

_____

_____

_____

12. When do you touch your breasts? In the morning when you wake up? At night before sleeping? In the shower or bath? When you're with another person? _____

_____

_____

_____

_____

13. On what other occasions do you touch them? _____

_____

_____

_____

_____

14. The French use the image of a woman with one bare breast storming the barricades to represent freedom. Now, theoretically, if you were to participate in this ritual, which of your breasts would you bare, and why? _____

_____

_____

_____

PART 9. DOUBLE-BREASTED

Angela coined this phrase, so this part is dedicated to her.

Meema Spadola writes in *Breasts*:

> There is no end to the lengths we can go in order to measure up to the next woman, only to find there's another woman with bigger, perkier, softer, rounder breasts.

1. In the past, have you ever been envious of another female's breasts? What was it like for you? _____

    _____

    _____

    _____

2. What part of this other ideal breast do you envision as yours? Shape? Size? Nipples? Color? Texture? Movement?

    _____

    _____

    _____

3. Have you seen in reality, the ideal breasts for you? Where? What are they like? _____

    _____

    _____

    _____

    _____

4. Was the female who had these ideal breasts aware of her assets? If so, what was her attitude?

    _____

    _____

    _____

5. Because of the look of your breasts, were you ever the subject of other women's curiosity or envy? What kind of feeling did it elicit in you? _____

    _____

    _____

    _____

    _____

    _____

    _____

6. Read the following from *Survival of the Prettiest,* by Nancy Etcoff, Ph.D., and try to figure out what it means:

    > In the United States breasts have become a major focus of erotic interest, an interest that has coincided with lower incidence of breast-feeding and with increased use of surgical techniques to mimic the nulliparous breast. It is interesting that in our lipophobic society, where fat has been demonized practically everywhere else here is still so much interest in acquiring and admiring these two mounded vessels plumped with fat.

    _____

    _____

    _____

    _____

    _____

    _____

    _____

    _____

    _____

    _____

PART 10. BREASTS AND FEARS

Pat spent her adult life deathly afraid of her breasts. She has overcome the fear, so this part is for her.

Rosie O'Donnell and Dr. Deborah Axelrod write in their book *Bosom Buddies,*

> Breast cancer remains by far the most common cancer among women worldwide, and the leading cause of death in American women aged forty to fifty-nine.

1. Have you ever witnessed a woman's struggle with and survival of breast cancer? _____

    _____

    _____

    _____

    _____

2. Have you been close to someone who has gone through the healing process? _____

    _____

    _____

    _____

    _____

3. Some women admit to a fear of breast cancer. Some believe that they will get sick in the future. Others are sure they will never get sick. Have you ever given it a thought? _____

    _____

    _____

    _____

    _____

4. What would you say or have said to a friend who finds out she has a lump in her breast? _____

_____

_____

_____

_____

5. What can you say to a friend who finds out her lump is malignant? _____

_____

_____

_____

_____

6. Have you heard survivors talk about their attitude toward their breasts? _____

_____

_____

_____

_____

7. What have you learned from the women who have had breast cancer? _____

_____

_____

_____

_____

8. Have you seen any changes in your attitude? _____

_____

_____

_____

_____

9.   List the names of women you have known who were diag-
     nosed with breast cancer. _____

     _____

     _____

     _____

     _____

     _____

     _____

10. Every one of us has known a woman who battled breast
     cancer. Some of us have known women whose husbands
     left them in mid-struggle. Do you know of these cases? Why
     do you think this happens? _____

     _____

     _____

     _____

     _____

     _____

     _____

     _____

PART 11.
BE YOUR OWN SEX THERAPIST

I dedicate this part to Lisa who wanted larger breasts for sexual and aesthetic reasons. She has since integrated sensuality and sexuality into her personal growth without objectifying her breasts.

Meema Spadola writes in *Breasts,*

> The link between breasts and mothering means that both men and women may treat breasts as a maternal object during lovemaking. This connection can be rewarding and comforting for some women.

1.   Are your breasts a sex organ to you? _____

_____

_____

_____

2.   Do you consider your breasts to be sexy? _____

_____

_____

_____

3.   In sexual play, do you like to think of your breasts as a major player? _____

_____

_____

_____

4.   It has often been said that most men don't know what to do with women's breasts. During lovemaking, do you prefer more breast play? Less? Or none? Explain. _____

_____

_____

_____

5.   Do you feel comfortable telling your partner how you want your breasts played with? What instructions will you give?

_____

_____

_____

_____

6.   In a nonsexual situation, are you aware of having breasts? Are there other emotions that you feel? Name them (from pride to shame). _____

_____

_____

_____

_____

7.   Are you aware of emphasizing your chest in certain social situations? _____

_____

_____

_____

_____

Business circumstances? _____

_____

_____

_____

Sexual play? _____

_____

_____

_____

_____

8.   Dr. Miriam Stoppard writes in *The Breast Book:*

It is curious, but nonetheless true, that there should be fashion in breast types. What remains constant, however, is women's use of the breasts as part of the armory of sex appeal.

Do you consider your breasts an important part of your sex appeal? If so, how important are they? _____

_____

_____

_____

_____

_____

_____

_____

_____

_____

PART 12.
BREAST CANCER SURVIVORS

We dedicate this part to the memory of Susan, Pat's mother, who died from breast cancer.

If you know a breast cancer survivor, or if you are one, please think about the following questions. Write down your responses.

1. Before you had breast cancer, what was your attitude towards your breasts? _____

    _____

    _____

    _____

2. Did you consider your breasts to be a symbol of femininity? Had they provided a certain status for you in the past? Do they now? _____

    _____

    _____

    _____

3. Before the diagnosis of breast cancer, did you like or dislike both breasts equally? Explain your feelings. _____

    _____

    _____

    _____

4. What advice do you have for others regarding prevention of breast cancer? _____

    _____

    _____

    _____

    _____

    _____

5. What have you learned about your own body image during these times: Before the diagnosis of breast cancer? _____

_____

_____

_____

_____

During treatments? _____

_____

_____

_____

_____

During recovery? _____

_____

_____

_____

_____

6. Following your recovery from breast cancer, what importance do breasts have in your life and how has that changed?

_____

_____

_____

As a woman, in general? _____

_____

_____

_____

As a mother?_____

_____

_____

_____

As a spouse or partner? _____

_____

_____

_____

_____

7.   What considerations, thoughts, or decisions did you make in regard to reconstructive surgery? _____

_____

_____

_____

_____

_____

_____

_____

_____

_____

_____

_____

_____

_____

_____

_____

PART 13.
THE AUGMENTED BREASTS

Nina is a friend of Beth. She had breast augmentation surgery. This part is dedicated to Nina and should be answered by anyone who has had this surgery.

1.   Why did you decide to have cosmetic breast surgery?

_____

_____

_____

_____

_____

2.   Was the medical experience everything you had expected?

_____

_____

_____

_____

_____

3.   Were the results what you had expected? Yes? No? Please explain. _____

_____

_____

_____

Are you satisfied with your breasts now? In what ways?

_____

_____

_____

If you are not satisfied, why not? _____

_____

_____

_____

_____

4. Do you notice a difference in your body image now compared with your body image before the surgery? If yes, what is the difference? _____

_____

_____

_____

5. Did you consider breasts to be a symbol for femininity? Had they provided a certain status for you in the past? Do they now? _____

_____

_____

_____

6. Before the breast augmentation surgery, did you like or dislike both breasts equally? Explain your feelings. _____

_____

_____

_____

7. What advice do you have for others who may want to change the size or shape of their breasts? _____

_____

_____

_____

_____

8. What importance do breasts have in your life now and how has that changed? _____

_____

_____

_____

As a woman, in general? _____

_____

_____

_____

_____

As a mother? _____

_____

_____

_____

_____

As a spouse or partner? _____

_____

_____

_____

_____

PART 14. THE QUIZ, AGAIN

This is the same quiz that you took at the beginning of these exercises. Please take it again and compare the results with those of the first quiz.

1. My mother has never shared with me her attitude about her own breasts.

    ❏ YES   ❏ NO

2. Watching breast-feeding in public is shameful and makes me uncomfortable.

    ❏ YES   ❏ NO

3. When in the presence of a woman, I am embarrassed when I am conscious of her breasts.

    ❏ YES   ❏ NO

4. I have never had a relationship with my breasts that I am aware of.

    ❏ YES   ❏ NO

5. I spend more time thinking about my hair, skin, nails, and heart than on the health of my breasts.

    ❏ YES   ❏ NO

6. I never respond in any way when I touch my breasts.

    ❏ YES   ❏ NO

7. Large-breasted women are more sexually responsive than small-breasted women.

    ❏ YES   ❏ NO

8. It is true that a woman's breast size correlates to her mothering abilities.

   ❏ YES   ❏ NO

9. Sagging breasts are a sign of diminished sexual excitement for a woman.

   ❏ YES   ❏ NO

10. I have sometimes been envious or obsessed with another woman's breasts.

    ❏ YES   ❏ NO

KEY

Now add up your YES responses and compare them with your first quiz. I hope you've improved!

0–2: Congratulations! You are booby-trapped-free. Keep it up.

3–4: You are somewhat booby-trapped. You need to improve your attitude.

5–7: Rethink your value system. You are potentially hurtful to others.

8–10: You are severely booby-trapped. Get help now!

You have probably improved your score
on this quiz. Congratulations!

PART 15.
A DAILY BREASTS MEDITATION

You may prerecord this meditation or have someone read it to you.

Sit comfortably, your legs and arms uncrossed, and take three long, slow, cleansing breaths.

Look at your chest.

On your chest, outside your rib cage, dwell these organs called breasts. Take a good look at them. Now close your eyes. Continue to breathe slowly. Look at your chest with the inner eyes of your mind. Let your mind's eyes see your real breasts. Relax. Breathe slowly and luxuriously. Take in lots of air and take your time.

Here, near your heart, are the organs we are meditating about. These are the same organs you first felt on your mother's chest as she held you, marveling over you minutes after you were born. They are also one of the first places where most of us were nourished as our mothers cradled us.

Relax. Breathe in generously and stretch your hands out. Now very slowly put your hands on your heart. Feel the life pumping there and enjoy the energy. This is the heart that you respect each day. You nurture its health, you are careful with its maintenance, and you attribute to it enormous responsibilities in your emotional life. Outside of your heart dwell your woman's breasts.

Continue to breathe slowly and relax. Enjoy the rhythmic pulse of your heart. Imagine those breasts again. They were not always with you, you know. For the first ten, eleven, twelve, or even thirteen years of your life, you did not have your breasts. One day they were budding. The next day they were blooming and blossoming. To some of us, they were growing faster than we did. To others, they stopped growing while our feet still increased in shoe size.

Listen to your heartbeat and notice your breasts. Those breasts are alive. Treat them well and they will help you stay healthy. Learn to accept them and love them. Remember these bosoms next to your heart. Practice and make them your friends. Your bosom's buddies. You know you cannot leave home without them. Take them everywhere with you with pride. And especially bring them home to your heart, in your consciousness. Carry them home lovingly as an integrated part of yourself.

Your breasts are not a symbolic artifact that stands in for femininity. Your breasts are living organs of your female body. Those human tissues that make a breast are very vulnerable parts of the female anatomy. Respect them. Check and test them frequently. Talk to them like you would to plants or pets or other lovely living things. Enjoy the softness of the skin that envelops your breasts and notice the texture of your nipples. Embrace them as you would your own child. In fact, give them a loving nickname.

And now it is time for a long hug from your loving arms to your beloved breasts. As you hug this pair of friends, thank them for being there, healthy and available for your needs.

When you are finished saying thank you, please open your eyes.

YOUR BREASTS' STORIES

YOUR BREASTS' STORIES

Character Index

This index provides the page number for each character, noting when they first appear, where their issues are mainly discussed, and where there is a significant development in their personal story.

References

Angier, Natalie, *Woman An Intimate Geography* (Houghton Mifflin, New York: 1999).

Angell, Marcia, M.D., *Science on Trial* (W.W. Norton, New York: 1996).

Arnot, Bob, M.D., *The Breast Cancer Prevention Diet* (Little, Brown & Company, Boston: 1998).

Brownmiller, Susan, *Femininity* (Fawcett Columbine, New York: 1984).

Breathnach, Sarah Ban, *Something More* (Warner Books, New York: 1998).

Brumberg, Joan Jacobs, *The Body Project* (Random House, New York: 1997).

Byrne, John, *Informed Consent* (McGraw-Hill, New York: 1996).

Etcoff, Nancy, *Survival of the Prettiest* (Doubleday, New York: 1999).

Gordon, Lori H., Ph.D., *Passages to Intimacy* (Fireside, New York: 1993).

Guthrie, Randolph H., M.D. with Doug Podolsky, *The Truth About Breast Implants* (John Wiley & Sons, New York: 1994).

Lewis, Michael, *Shame: The Exposed Self* (The Free Press, New York: 1995).

Love, Susan, M.D., *Dr. Susan Love's Breast Book* (Addison Wesley, New York: 1995).

Masterson, James F., M.D., *The Personality Disorders* (Zeig, Tucker & Company, Phoenix, Ariz.: 2000).

Morrison, Andrew, *Shame: The Underside of Narcissism* (The Analitic Press, Hillsdale, N.J.: 1989).

Nash, Jennie, *The Victoria's Secret Catalog Never Stops Coming* (Scriber, New York: 2001).

Northrup, Christiane, M.D., *Women's Bodies, Women's Wisdom* (Bantam Books, New York: 1999).

———*The Wisdom of Menopause* (Bantam Books, New York: 2001).

O'Donnell, Rosie and Deborah Axelrod, M.D., *Bosom Buddies* (Warner Books, New York: 1999).

Prose, Francine, Karen Finley, Dario Fo, and Charles Simic, *Master Breasts* (Aperture Foundation, Inc., Ontario: 1998).

Reese, L., J. Wilkinson, P. Koppelman, eds., *I'm on My Way Running: Women Speaking on Coming of Age* (Avon Books, New York: 1983).

Reiss, Uzzi, M.D./OB-GYN with Martin Zucker, *Natural Hormone Balance for Women* (Pocket Books, New York: 2001).

Rosenthal, M. Sara, *The Breast Sourcebook* (Lowell House, Los Angeles: 1996).

Rosoff, Ilene, *The Woman Source Catalog and Review.* (Celestial Arts, Berkeley: 1996).

Rothenberg, Robert E., *The Complete Book of Breast Care* (Crown Publishers, New York: 1975).

Sarrel, Lorna J., M.S.W., and Phillip M. Sarrel, M.D., *Sexual Unfolding* (Little, Brown & Company, Boston: 1979).

Schaef, Anne Wilson, *When Society Becomes Addictive* (Harper Collins, New York: 1987).

Spadola, Meema, *Breasts* (Wildcat Canyon Press, Berkeley: 1998).

Stoppard, Miriam, M.D., *The Breast Book* (Carroll & Brown Limited, London: 1996).

Stoller, Robert J., M.D., *Presentation of Gender* (Yale University Press, New York: 1985).

———*Observing the Erotic Imagination* (Yale University Press, New Haven, Conn. and London: 1985).

Wadler, Joyce, *My Breast* (Pocket Books, New York: 1992).

Wolf, Naomi, *The Beauty Myth* (Anchor Books, New York: 1991).

Yalom, Marilyn, *A History of the Breast* (Ballantine, New York: 1997).

Index

A

Amazons, 185
American Cancer Society, 147
Amy (Grace's daughter), 9, 33, 191–192, 194–195, 221
Angela, 10, 15, 47–49, 81–83, 97–100, 104–106, 110–117, 135–137, 176, 197, 235
Angell, Marcia, 72–73
Angier, Natalie, 223
asymmetry, breasts, xi, 51
attitude of femininity, 5
Axelrod, Deborah, 151, 163–164, 237

B

babies, size of as proof of femininity, 59
beauty as subjective experience, 123–124
Beauty Myth, The (Wolf), 106
Beth, 9, 13, 21, 26–27, 47, 124, 180–181, 187–189, 197, 207
Bioenergetic therapy, 17
body decorations, 133–134
body manipulations, 4, 5, 121–138
body parts, preoccupation with, 81–83
Body Project, The (Brumberg), 80–82, 83, 86–87
booby-trapped
    concept of, 138
    as discussion topic, 182, 187
    as range of attitudes, 210–211
    therapy group members, 195–199
Bosom Buddies (O'Donnell and Axelrod), 151, 163–164, 237
bosom buddies system, 213
bras
    attitudes and feelings about, 228–231
    handmade projects, 84–86
    history of, 83
    perspectives on use, 87
"Brassiere, The" (Fournel), 224
Breast Book, The (Stoppard), 242

breast cancer, 51, 144, 148–154, 163–164, 167–170, 237–239
breast cancer survivors, 243–245
breast dialogues, 117–118
breast-feeding, 6, 33, 189–192, 218–223
breast implants, 5–6, 26–27, 163, 180–183, 187–189, 246–248
Breastology, 53, 101
breasts
    and American culture, 69–70
    anthropological issues of development, 79–82
    appreciation for, 6
    double breasted, 105–106, 211–212, 235–236
    and fears, 237–239
    language and terminology, 210–214
    myths and realities, 215–217
    naming, 90–91
    "normal" breasts, 49, 53
    physical characteristics, 49–53
    physical development of, 225–227
    reactions to viewing others' breasts, 53–57
    relationships with, 88–93, 138, 179–180, 207–209, 232–234
    and sexual attractiveness, 65–69, 240–242
    size and hormones, 51–52
    women's specific concerns about, 3
breasts' asymmetry, xi, 51
Breasts (Spadola), 235, 240
Brumberg, Joan Jacobs, 80–82, 83, 86–87
Byrne, John, 75–76

C

chicken soup preparation, 109–110, 116, 117
Chinese feet wrapping, 121–123
circumcision
    of females, 128
    of males, 125–127, 133

About the Author

Dr. Nili Sachs is a marriage and family therapist with a doctorate degree in clinical psychology for nearly three decades, dividing her practice between Los Angeles and Minneapolis.

Born in Tel-Aviv, Israel, Nili is a certified physical education teacher. Those skills of understanding the human body and its dynamics propelled her constant journey of discovery and rediscovery.

Dr. Nili Sachs (Shalev) is the author of *Yerida Medaat*, published in Hebrew in 1991 by Modan, a major publishing house in Tel-Aviv. This book describes the emotional turmoil of immigrants to the United States, their culture shock, and their long process of acculturation and adjustment. The greatest impact this book has is on immigrants who are parents and their evolving relationships with their "Americanized" children.

Her book tour included Israel's Media and major North American cities. As a result of the demand for her original and well researched material, Nili developed and produced a videotape/lecture called: *Children of Immigrants* and was an advisor on a TV documentary *Where is Home?*, both based on her book.

In her private practice Dr. Nili Sachs specializes in facilitating seminars for couples and singles, focusing on issues such as intimacy, sensuality, fidelity; spirituality and the inter-connections among them.

Dr. Nili Sachs is a certified leader for the acclaimed international programs P.A.I.R.S. (Practical Application of Intimate Relationship Skills), and is a recipient of PAIRS International's Raving Fans Award.

Dr. Sachs advised and trained the lead actors of the MGM movie *Time Bomb*, released in 1989 in Europe. The film dealt with the mental anguish and fear inflicted by terrorists and the psychological treatment of Post Traumatic Stress Disorder.

She also hosted a weekly TV segment on family life, parenting, relationships and relevant mental health topics on a syndicated cable program, originated in Los Angeles.

For several years Dr. Nili contributed to her monthly column on human sexuality and intimacy matters in a women's magazine. She also contributed to her weekly column in a newspaper.

For corporations and associations, Dr. Sachs consults and delivers keynotes and seminars on subjects such as sexual harassment, gender communication, women's wellness, relationships and marriage.

As for professional memberships, Dr. Nili Sachs is a Clinical Member of the American Association of Marriage and Family Therapists, and an active Professional Member in the National Speakers Association.

From early on Nili enjoyed studying and understanding people's behaviors and actions under unusual human conditions. Thus her interests in women serving in the armed forces became a special interest for her as she served in the Israeli Defense Forces as a physical education instructor. In the same vein, observing the mental health of immigrants and their family interactions became subject for research.

However, the most exotic journeys Dr. Nili participated in were two amazing anthropological expeditions. The first one occurred in 1988 into the jungles of Ecuador, along the Amazon river, to observe the life and rituals of the native Indians, to witness an exorcism by an Indian Shaman, and to find out about their family structure and customs. Her second expedition, in 1990, took her to the jungles of Borneo, Indonesia, were she volunteered to nurture orphan Orangutans back to the wild. Those experiences left a remarkable emotional, physical and spiritual impression on her, as it is well reflected in the materials she brings to her audiences.

In her new book *Booby-Trapped*, Dr. Nili integrates her knowledge of the human body and its dynamics with her clinical observations on concerns such as body-image, perceptions of femininity/masculinity, and the mind/body/spirit connection.

In 2003 Dr. Nili participated with a panel of experts in a movie-length documentary: *Boobs, an American Obsession*, a WhirlieGirl Production. The documentary explores the newest procedures as well as preoccupation with breast augmentations in the US.

Nili's favorite daily pursuits continue to be reading and exercising, especially in the Pilates method.

She is married, has two sons and one grandson.

Other Books by Nili Sachs, Ph.D.

Yerida Medaat

(In Hebrew)
Publisher: Modan House, Tel Aviv, Israel
Hardcover, 1991

Yerida Medaat is a psychological study of immigrants to the US.

In her book Dr. Sachs (Shalev) is exploring the effect immigration has on individuals, married couples and families.

This book describes the emotional turmoil of immigrants to the United States, their culture shock, and their long process of acculturation and adjustment. The greatest impact this book has is on immigrants who are parents and their evolving relationships with their "Americanized" children.

Treasured Chest

A personal workbook.

This workbook helps the reader see the bigger picture of attitudes and history of her relationships with her own breasts.

Treasured Chest includes anecdotes and contributions from readers of *Booby-Trapped*.

Contact Information

For more information about booking Dr. Nili Sachs for speaking to your organization, or for consultation:

9091 County Road 50
P.O. Box 44
Rockford, MN 55373
Phone: 888-471-3730
Fax: 952-471-3732

Email: *DrNili@boobytrapped.com*
www.boobytrapped.com

To obtain a subscription to the Booby-Trapped Newsletter, visit:

www.boobytrapped.com

Tell a friend!

For Foreign Rights
Contact:

InterLicense, LTD.

110 Country Club Drive #A

Mill Valley, CA 94941   USA

tel (415) 381-9780

Fax (415) 381-6485

Email: *ilicense@aol.com*